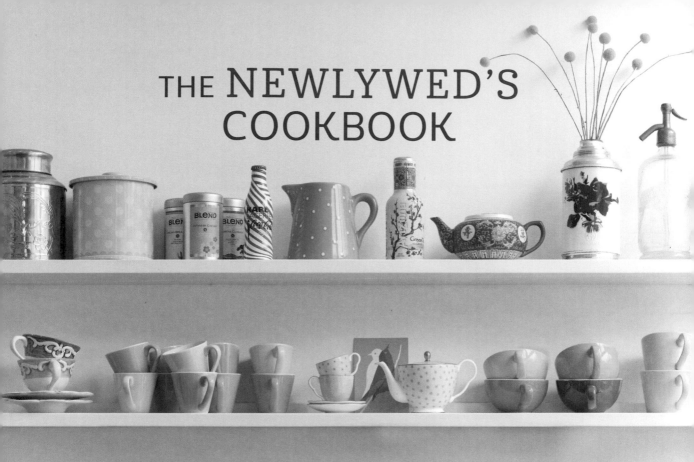

THE NEWLYWED'S COOKBOOK

Fresh and modern recipes to cook and share together

RYLAND PETERS & SMALL
LONDON • NEW YORK

Senior Designer Toni Kay
Editor Miriam Catley
Production Controller David Hearn
Art Director Leslie Harrington
Editorial Director Julia Charles
Publisher Cindy Richards
Indexer Vanessa Bird

First published in 2019 by
Ryland Peters & Small
20–21 Jockey's Fields, London
WC1R 4BW
and
341 E 116th St, New York NY 10029
www.rylandpeters.com

10 9 8 7 6 5 4 3 2 1

Text copyright © Valerie Aikman-Smith,
Jordan Bourke, Felipe Fuentes Cruz
& Ben Fordham, Dunja Gulin, Kathy
Kordalis, Jenny Linford, Nitisha Patel,
James Porter, Shelagh Ryan, Laura
Santtini, Milli Taylor and Jenny
Tschiesche.

Design and photographs copyright
© Ryland Peters & Small 2019

ISBN: 978-1-78879-064-2

Printed in China

The authors' moral rights have been
asserted. All rights reserved. No part
of this publication may be reproduced,
stored in a retrieval system or
transmitted in any form or by any
means, electronic, mechanical,
photocopying or otherwise, without
the prior permission of the publisher.

A CIP record for this book is available
from the British Library.

US Library of Congress Cataloging-in-
Publication Data has been applied for.

NOTES:
• Both British (Metric) and American
(Imperial plus US cups) measurements
are included in these recipes for your
convenience, however it is important to
work with one set of measurements and not
alternate between the two within a recipe.
• All spoon measurements are level
unless otherwise specified.
• All eggs are medium (UK) or large (US),
unless specified as large, in which case
US extra-large should be used. Uncooked
eggs should not be served to the very old,
frail, young children, pregnant women or
those with compromised immune systems.
• Ovens should be preheated to the
specified temperatures. We recommend
using an oven thermometer. If using a
fan-assisted oven, adjust temperatures
according to the manufacturer's
instructions.
• When a recipe calls for the grated
zest of citrus fruit, buy unwaxed fruit
and wash well before using. If you can
only find treated fruit, scrub well in
warm soapy water before using.

CONTENTS

INTRODUCTION

Starting out on married life means enjoying time together at home, cooking good food for yourselves and your loved ones, whether it's friends or your recently extended family. The idea of eating and entertaining together in your new life can be a little daunting, no matter how much cooking you have done in the past. Here is the ultimate helping hand in the form of a carefully selected collection of recipes. Quick and healthy breakfasts, deliciously indulgent brunch ideas for lazy weekend lie-ins, nutritious salads that can be whipped up and packed to take to work, delicious dinners for two to serve up when spending quality time together plus smart ideas for effortless entertaining. From impressive freshly-baked bread to sheet-pan saviours, quick and easy pastas to indulgent Sunday roasts – all the recipes you will ever need are here.

Whatever you want to cook and share, this go-to source of inspiration will make eating together a pleasure time and time again and it will find a place on the kitchen bookshelf for years to come.

From within these pages you can compile a menu to suit any occasion. Here are just a few menu suggestions:

BREAKFAST
& BRUNCH

QUINOA GRANOLA, TROPICAL FRUIT & COCONUT YOGURT

*A nourishing gluten- and refined sugar-free granola,
served on coconut yogurt with fruit.*

papaya, pineapple,
  and mango slices
2 passion fruits, halved
200 g/1 cup coconut
  milk yogurt, such
  as Coyo
150 g/1 cup quinoa
  granola (see below)
coconut blossom
  syrup, to serve

GRANOLA
200 g/2 cups quinoa
  flakes
2 tablespoons ground
  flaxseeds
1 tablespoon chia
  seeds (optional)
50 g/scant ½ cup
  macadamia nuts,
  roughly chopped

50 g/scant ½ cup
  pistachio nuts,
  roughly chopped
50 g/scant ½ cup
  cashew nuts,
  roughly chopped
4 tablespoons coconut
  blossom syrup
1 tablespoon apple
  juice
1 teaspoon vanilla
  paste
30 g/¾ cup coconut
  chips, lightly toasted

SERVES 6

Preheat the oven to 180°C (350°F) Gas 4.

To make the granola, put the quinoa flakes,
ground flaxseeds, chia seeds (if using) and
the nuts in a large bowl and mix together.
Stir in the coconut blossom syrup, apple
juice and vanilla paste. Spread the mixture
onto a baking sheet lined with parchment
paper and bake in the preheated oven for
10 minutes. Break up the mixture with a fork
and bake for a futher 10 minutes. Remove
from the oven and stir in the coconut chips.
Allow to cool. Store in an airtight container
for up to a month (this keeps well so you
may wish to double up on the quantities).

Arrange the fruit on small plates. Put a
few spoonfuls of the coconut yogurt and
the granola into small glass bowls, add a
coconut blossom syrup and serve. Serve
with a Pomini cocktail for a special treat
(page 150).

BIRCHER MUESLI WITH FRESH BERRIES

A fantastic alternative to porridge for summer, this is one of those recipes that can be modified ad infinitum. Try substituting the apple juice with orange or cranberry, add pumpkin seeds, macadamia nuts, dried apricots or any dried or poached fruit.

250 g/1¼ cups jumbo
   rolled oats
30 g/⅓ cup (dark)
   raisins
375 ml/1½ cups apple
   juice
30 g/⅓ cup whole
   almonds
freshly squeezed juice
   and grated zest of
   ½ lemon
1 apple or pear,
   coarsely grated
125 ml/½ cup yogurt
mixed fresh berries,
   to serve
clear honey, to serve

SERVES 4

Place the oats and raisins in a large mixing bowl and pour over the apple juice. Cover with clingfilm/plastic wrap and chill in the fridge for at least an hour, preferably overnight.

Preheat the oven to 180°C (350°F) Gas 4.

Scatter the almonds onto a baking sheet greased and lined with parchment paper and toast in the preheated oven for about 10 minutes. Remove from the oven and set aside to cool before chopping to a rough texture.

Remove the soaked oat mixture from the fridge. Uncover and add the lemon juice and zest, chopped toasted almonds and grated apple or pear. Stir to combine.

Add the yogurt, a little at a time, stirring after each addition to your desired consistency.

Serve in bowls with fresh berries on top and a drizzle of honey.

APPLE PANCAKES

These are quick to make and can be made gluten-free. The combination of the light nuttiness of the buckwheat, the tartness of the apple and the mellow sweetness of the maple syrup is a winner.

150 g/1 heaping cup
   gluten-free plain/
   all-purpose flour
100 g/¾ cup
   buckwheat flour
1 tablespoon caster/
   granulated sugar
1 teaspoon gluten-free
   baking powder
a pinch of salt
1 egg
220 ml/scant 1 cup milk
½ teaspoon vanilla
   paste
butter, for frying
1 Granny Smith apple,
   cored, peeled and
   sliced into circles
maple syrup, yogurt,
   vanilla powder and
   blackberries,
   to serve

MAKES 8

Put the flours, sugar, baking powder and salt in a bowl and make a well in the centre. Crack the egg in the middle and pour in one-quarter of the milk. Use a whisk to combine the mixture thoroughly. Once you have a paste, mix in another quarter of the milk and, when all the lumps are gone, mix in the remaining milk and the vanilla paste. Leave to rest for 20 minutes. Stir again before cooking.

Heat a small non-stick frying pan/skillet and add a knob/pat of butter. When the butter starts to foam, ladle the pancake mixture into the centre of the pan forming a circle, then place an apple ring in the centre. Cook for a few minutes until golden brown on the bottom and the bubbles are bursting on the surface of the pancake, then turn over and cook until golden on the other side. Repeat until you have used all the mixture, stirring the mixture between pancakes and adding more butter for frying as necessary.

Serve with maple syrup, yogurt, vanilla powder and blackberries.

ALL-IN-ONE BREAKFAST

You'll need just five ingredients for this simple one pan dish. It's a delicious twist on the traditional breakfast of bacon and eggs and so quick to prepare you'll make it all the time.

4 large field mushrooms
2 tablespoons olive oil
12 slices Parma ham/
    prosciutto or
    bresaola
4 eggs
1 tablespoon freshly
    chopped parsley
sea salt and freshly
    ground black pepper

SERVES 2

Preheat the oven to 220°C (425°F) Gas 7.

Place the mushrooms on a baking sheet with sides. Drizzle over the olive oil and season with salt and pepper.

Bake in the preheated oven for 15 minutes. Check that the mushrooms are almost cooked through. If not, cook for up to a further 5 minutes.

Add the ham or bresaola to the sheet pan and crack the eggs on top.

Bake for another 7–10 minutes until the eggs are just cooked.

Remove from the oven, sprinkle over the fresh parsley and enjoy.

SCRAMBLED EGGS WITH CHANTERELLES

This simple but luxurious combination makes a wonderful breakfast or brunch dish.

100 g/3½ oz. fresh chanterelle mushrooms
4 eggs
1 tablespoon butter, plus extra for the toast
1 tablespoon olive oil
2 slices of freshly made toast
salt and freshly ground black pepper
freshly chopped parsley, to garnish (optional)

SERVES 2

Trim down the stalks of the chanterelle mushrooms and halve any large ones.

Beat the eggs together in a bowl and season with salt and freshly ground black pepper.

Heat the butter in small, heavy saucepan. Add the beaten egg and cook over a low heat, stirring often, until scrambled.

Meanwhile, heat the olive oil in a frying pan/skillet. Add the chanterelles and fry over a high heat for 2–3 minutes, until lightly browned and softened. Season with salt and freshly ground black pepper.

Spread the toast with butter, top with the scrambled eggs and then the fried chanterelles. Serve at once, garnished with freshly chopped parsley.

PROSCIUTTO EGGS

This is a cheat's fancy ham and egg and a nice way to serve it for brunch.

6 slices of prosciutto
6 eggs
6 sprigs of thyme
a handful of grated Parmesan (optional)
sea salt and freshly ground black pepper
6-hole muffin pan, greased with vegetable oil

MAKES 6

Preheat the oven to 200°C (400°F) Gas 6.

Line the prepared muffin pan with prosciutto and place in the preheated oven for 5 minutes. Using two spoons, pull the prosciutto back against the sides of the muffin holes. Crack an egg into each prosciutto-lined muffin hole and top with a sprig of thyme and a pinch of Parmesan. Bake in the preheated oven for 10–15 minutes or until set. Remove from the oven and take out of their moulds. Serve with freshly ground black pepper and salt.

CAULIFLOWER, BUTTERNUT & KALE HASH

So delicious and good for you too! You could eat any leftovers for supper with a poached egg and a dash of sriracha sauce for extra kick.

1 tablespoon olive oil
2 tablespoons butter
1 onion, roughly chopped
1 garlic clove, crushed
½ cauliflower, cut into bitesize pieces
150 g/5½ oz. butternut squash, peeled
    and cut into bitesize pieces
a handful of kale, stems removed, leaves
    roughly chopped
2 tablespoons finely chopped chives
grated Parmesan (optional)
sea salt and freshly ground black pepper

SERVES 6

Heat the olive oil and butter in a large frying pan/skillet. Add the onion and garlic and cook for 5 minutes. Add the cauliflower and squash, season with salt and pepper and cook over a medium heat for 20 minutes, stirring regularly.

Add the kale and cook for a further 10 minutes. The pan should have enough space for each vegetable to colour really well, and if they catch a little – even better. Once cooked through and caramelized, check the seasoning and add salt and pepper if necessary. Top with the chives and Parmesan, if using, and serve.

SWEET POTATO, PEA & MINT FRITTERS

Not only can these fritters be served at brunch, but they're also brilliant as a side dish with meat, poultry or fish for dinner or in a wrap with salad for lunch.

2 eggs
1 sweet potato, peeled, grated and
    squeezed of moisture
80 g/½ cup petit pois
2 spring onions/scallions, chopped
3 tablespoons plain/all-purpose flour
4 sprigs of mint, leaves removed
    and chopped
1 tablespoon olive oil
coconut oil, for frying
sea salt and freshly ground black pepper

MAKES 10–12

Whisk the eggs well in a small bowl. Combine with the sweet potato, peas, spring onions/scallions, flour, mint, olive oil and salt and pepper to taste, mixing well.

In a large pan, melt the coconut oil over a medium heat. Spoon in the potato mixture, 1 heaping tablespoon at a time, and pat down into a flat patty with a spatula. Cook for 4 minutes on each side until golden and crispy. Remove from the pan with a spatula, drain on paper towels and serve.

AVOCADO WHIP

This avo whip has a smoothness to it and works nicely as a dip. For a much creamier and fluffier consistency, use a Nutribullet-type blender – it's worth it. But if you are in the more chunky avo brigade, coarsely chop all the ingredients instead.

2 avocados, peeled and stoned/pitted
a handful of spinach
a handful of parsley
juice of 1 lemon
30 ml/2 tablespoons olive oil
sea salt and freshly ground black pepper

SERVES 6

In a food processor, blitz the avocado, spinach, parsley, lemon juice, olive oil and salt and pepper into a smooth, light and fluffy paste. Transfer to a bowl to serve.

CORN FRITTERS WITH ROAST TOMATOES & SMASHED AVOCADOS

150 g/2 cups (about 1 medium) grated courgette/zucchini
sea salt and freshly ground black pepper, to season
400 g/2½ cups cherry vine tomatoes
olive oil, to drizzle
4 eggs
180 g/1⅓ cups self-raising/rising flour
50 g/1¾ oz. Parmesan, grated
100 ml/scant ½ cup buttermilk
1 teaspoon paprika
½ teaspoon cayenne pepper
1 tablespoon chopped coriander/cilantro
fresh corn kernels cut from 2–3 cobs
sunflower oil, for frying
fresh spinach, to serve
crème fraîche, to serve

SMASHED AVOCADOS
3 avocados
freshly squeezed juice of 2 limes and the grated zest of 1
¼ red onion, finely diced
1 teaspoon hot sauce

SERVES 6

Corn fritters are a popular brunch menu staple. No two recipes are ever the same as everyone has their (strong!) opinion on what makes the perfect fritter.

Put the grated courgette/zucchini into a colander set over a large mixing bowl. Sprinkle with ½ teaspoon of salt and leave for 30 minutes–1 hour so they release their moisture. Squeeze the grated courgette/zucchini with your hands to get rid of as much moisture as possible and set aside.

For the roast tomatoes, preheat the oven to 180°C (350°F) Gas 4. Place the tomatoes on a baking sheet, drizzle with olive oil and season with salt and pepper.

Roast in the preheated oven for 15–20 minutes, or until the skins begin to split.

Reduce the oven temperature to 170°C (325°F) Gas 3 and prepare the fritter batter. In a large, clean, dry mixing bowl, lightly whisk the eggs. Add in the flour, grated Parmesan, buttermilk, paprika, cayenne pepper, ½ teaspoon of salt, a pinch of pepper and chopped coriander/cilantro.

Stir in the squeezed courgette/zucchini and corn kernels, ensuring the vegetables are evenly coated in batter.

Add enough sunflower oil to thinly cover the bottom of a heavy-bottomed frying pan/skillet. Ladle generous spoonfuls of batter into the pan and cook for about 4 minutes on each side, until golden brown. Transfer to a clean baking sheet and put in the still-warm oven for 4–5 minutes to ensure they are cooked through. Cook the remaining batter in the same way, adding a little more oil to the pan each time, if required.

Just before serving, roughly mash the avocados with a fork, leaving them fairly chunky. Stir in the lime juice and zest, onion and hot sauce. Season generously with salt and serve with the fritters, roast tomatoes, a handful of fresh spinach and a dollop of crème fraîche.

MEALS
FOR TWO

TOMATO SOUP WITH FENNEL, GARLIC & BASIL DRIZZLE

Tomato and basil are a classic summer flavour combination. The green basil oil provides a vibrant colour contrast to the orange-red of the soup base and elevates this humble tomato soup to something a little more refined.

1 bulb of garlic
olive oil, for roasting
350 g/10 oz. (about
   1 large) fennel bulb,
   trimmed and
   quartered
sea salt and freshly
   ground black pepper,
   to season
1 leek (white part only),
   roughly chopped
100 g/¾ cup (about
   2 sticks) chopped
   celery
150 g/1¼ cup (about
   1 medium) chopped
   carrot
500 g/2½ cups (about
   4 medium) roughly
   chopped tomatoes
1 x 400-g/14-oz. can
   plum tomatoes
500 ml/2 cups
   vegetable stock
15 g/¼ cup fresh basil

BASIL OIL
150 ml/⅔ cup olive oil,
   plus extra if needed
60 g/1 cup fresh basil
sea salt, to taste

SERVES 2

Preheat the oven to 200°C (400°F) Gas 6.

To roast the garlic, cut the top part off the top of the garlic head to expose the individual garlic cloves. Place the garlic head, cut-side down, onto a square piece of foil and drizzle with 2 teaspoons of olive oil. Lift the foil up around the garlic and place on a baking sheet. Roast in the preheated oven for 45 minutes. Remove from the oven, open the foil wrap and set aside to cool. When the garlic is cool enough to handle, squeeze the cloves out of the skin, coarsely chop the garlic flesh and discard the skin.

Place the quartered fennel in a roasting pan, drizzle with 1 tablespoon of olive oil and season with the salt and freshly ground black pepper. Cook in the same oven as the garlic for 25 minutes, or until you can easily insert the tip of a sharp knife into the flesh. Remove from the oven, set aside to cool slightly then roughly chop.

To make the basil oil, whizz together a little of the olive oil with the fresh basil and salt in a food processor. With the motor running, slowly drizzle in more oil until you have a loose, flavoured oil. Set aside until ready to serve.

Heat 2 tablespoons of olive oil in a large saucepan or pot set over a medium heat. Add the chopped leek, celery and carrot and gently cook for 10–15 minutes, stirring from time to time, until the vegetables are soft.

Add the roast garlic and fennel, fresh and canned tomatoes and vegetable stock. Bring the mixture to the boil then reduce the heat and simmer for 45 minutes.

Remove the pan from the heat, stir in the basil leaves and purée with a handheld electric mixer or in a food processor.

Season to taste and serve with a good drizzle of basil oil, some freshly ground black pepper, and garnish with fresh basil leaves.

GRILLED HALLOUMI WITH ROAST SHALLOTS, BEETROOT & VINCOTTO

50 g/½ cup pecans, toasted

25 g/½ cup flat-leaf parsley

2 tablespoons olive oil

250 g/9 oz. halloumi, cut into 1-cm/⅜-in. slices

freshly squeezed juice of ½ a lemon

sea salt and freshly ground black pepper, to season

ROAST BEETROOT

750 g/1 lb. 9 oz. (about 4 medium) beetroots/beets

2 tablespoons olive oil

1 tablespoon vincotto (or 1 tablespoon each of balsamic vinegar and clear honey)

1 teaspoon fennel seeds

ROAST SHALLOTS

300 g/2 cups peeled and quartered shallots

1 tablespoon olive oil

½ tablespoon vincotto

DRESSING

2 teaspoons vincotto

2 tablespoons olive oil

1 teaspoon clear honey

1 garlic clove, crushed

SERVES 2

Vincotto is a naturally sweet, 'cooked wine' syrup that can be used in both sweet and savoury dishes. It pairs beautifully with the salty halloumi cheese and earthy beetroot/beet in this salad. If you can't find vincotto you can substitute balsamic vinegar with a little honey. Like wine, vincottos vary a lot in quality so buy the best that you can find.

Begin by preparing the beetroots/beets. Put them in a saucepan or pot of boiling water and cook for about 40 minutes, until just tender. Drain and set aside to cool.

Once cold enough to handle, peel and cut into wedges.

Preheat the oven to 180°C (350°F) Gas 4.

Place the beetroot/beet wedges in a large mixing bowl with the oil, vincotto (or substitute) and fennel seeds. Toss to ensure everything is well-coated, then spread out on a baking sheet. Season with salt and pepper and roast in the preheated oven for 30 minutes.

Put the shallots in a large mixing bowl with the oil and vincotto (or substitute). Toss together and spread out on a baking sheet. Season with salt and pepper and roast in the preheated oven for about 15 minutes, until soft.

To make the vincotto dressing, place the vincotto, oil, honey and crushed garlic in a clean screw-top jar. Close the jar and shake. Season with salt and pepper and set aside.

Place the roast beetroot/beets, roast shallots, pecans and parsley in a large mixing bowl and gently toss together with the dressing and set aside until ready to serve.

Heat the oil in a large frying pan/skillet and fry the halloumi slices for 2 minutes on each side, until golden brown. Remove from the pan and drain on paper towels.

Serve the roast vegetable salad in bowls with the halloumi arranged on top. Squeeze the lemon juice over the cheese and enjoy.

HARISSA-BAKED AVOCADO, BUTTERNUT SQUASH & EGGS

The addition of spicy harissa to the already colourful flavour and texture combination of green avocado, bright orange butternut squash and eggs, is the ideal way to marry all of these ingredients together. It's rich and tangy in flavour, but the mellowness of the other ingredients contrasts well.

2 tablespoons harissa
   paste
2 tablespoons olive oil
550 g/1¼ lb. butternut
   squash, peeled,
   deseeded and
   roughly chopped into
   2-cm/¾-in. cubes
60 g/½ cup pitted/
   stoned black olives
15 cherry tomatoes
1 ripe avocado, peeled,
   pitted/stoned and
   thinly sliced
freshly squeezed juice
   of 1 lemon
4 UK large/
   US extra-large eggs
freshly ground black
   pepper

SERVES 2

Preheat the oven to 200°C (400°F) Gas 6.

Stir together the harissa paste and olive oil in a large bowl then toss in the butternut squash and stir again to coat the squash.

Put the butternut squash on a baking pan with sides and bake in the preheated oven for 30 minutes.

Meanwhile, prepare the avocado and squeeze over the lemon juice to prevent it from turning brown. After 30 minutes, add the olives, tomatoes and avocado to the butternut squash and bake for a further 10 minutes.

Make four wells in the vegetables and crack in the eggs. Bake for another 6–9 minutes until the egg whites are cooked. Season with freshly ground black pepper and serve.

TRIPLE TOMATO PIZZA

Homemade pizza is fun to make and to eat. This simple recipe offers a classic combination of flavours: the fresh acidity of tomatoes, mild mozzarella and salty anchovies.

500 g/4 cups strong
  bread flour
1 teaspoon caster/
  granulated sugar
1 teaspoon salt
1 teaspoon fast-action
  dried yeast
300 ml/1¼ cups
  lukewarm water
2 tablespoons olive oil
300 ml/1¼ cups tomato
  passata/strained
  tomatoes
8 sun-dried or sun-blush
  tomatoes in oil,
  chopped
8 cherry tomatoes,
  halved
2 balls fresh mozzarella,
  chopped
8 anchovy fillets in oil
  (each about
  10 g/⅓ oz.)
fresh basil leaves,
  to garnish
*a large mixing bowl,
  oiled*
*4 pizza stones or baking
  sheets, lightly floured*

MAKES 4

First, make the pizza dough. Mix together the flour, sugar, salt and yeast. Gradually, pour in the lukewarm water and the oil, forming a sticky dough. Turn out onto a lightly floured surface and knead until smooth and elastic. Transfer to the prepared mixing bowl, cover with a clean damp kitchen cloth and set aside in a warm place to rise for 1 hour.

Preheat the oven to 240°C (475°F) Gas 9.

Break down the pizza dough and roll out on a lightly floured surface to form 4 pizza bases.

Transfer each base to the prepared pizza stones or baking sheets. You may have to bake one at a time, depending on the size of your oven. Spread with tomato passata/strained tomatoes, leaving a rim of plain dough around the edge. Top each pizza with the sun-dried tomatoes, cherry tomatoes, mozzarella cheese and anchovy fillets.

Bake the pizzas in the preheated oven for 10–15 minutes until the mozzarella cheese has melted and the dough is golden. Sprinkle with basil leaves and serve at once. If you can't eat two you could pack them for lunch the next day.

UMAMI STEAKS WITH WILD MUSHROOMS

This simple but luxurious dish is a great way to enjoy wild mushrooms.

2 sirloin steaks, each approx. 150 g/5 oz. and 2-cm/¾-in. thick, at room temperature
1 tablespoons olive oil
2 tablespoons ground dried porcini (cep powder)
100 g/3½ oz. assorted wild mushrooms, such as chanterelles and porcini, or assorted cultivated mushrooms
salt and freshly ground black pepper

SERVES 2

Coat the steaks thoroughly in half of the olive oil, then coat well in the dried porcini powder on both sides. Season with salt and freshly ground black pepper.

Trim the wild mushrooms. If using cultivated mushrooms, cut them into 5-mm/³⁄₁₆-inch-thick slices.

Heat a griddle pan/ridged stovetop grill pan until very hot. Cook the steaks on the pan to your taste, turning over during the process. For medium-rare, allow around 2 minutes on each side.

Meanwhile, heat a heavy-based frying pan/skillet until hot. Add the remaining olive oil and heat through. Fry the wild mushrooms briefly over a high heat, until just browned and slightly softened. Season with salt and freshly ground black pepper. Serve each steak topped with a portion of the sautéed wild mushrooms.

VODKA PASTA

A perfect late night dish. For more vodka flavour, you can add it when the sauce is bubbling and just before you add the peas and remove the pan from the heat. This means that very little of the alcohol burns off and the taste of vodka will be very strong.

30 g/¼ stick butter

80 g/3 oz. cooked ham, cut into bite-size strips

125 ml/½ cup vodka

250 ml/1 cup double/ heavy cream

½ tablespoon tomato purée/paste, preferably Bomba!

a handful of frozen peas, defrosted

200 g/7 oz. dried pasta or 160 g/6 oz. fresh pasta

salt and freshly ground black pepper

2 tablespoons finely grated Parmigiano Reggiano, to serve

SERVES 2

First, make the sauce. Melt the butter in a large sauté pan. Add the ham and sauté until crispy. Add the vodka, cream and tomato purée/paste. When the mixture begins bubbling, add the peas and remove from the heat. Season to taste.

Bring a large pan of salted water to a rolling boil, add the pasta and cook according to the instructions on the packet.

Drain the pasta but keep a cup of the cooking water.

Tip the hot drained pasta into the creamy sauce. Toss with gusto over a high heat until the pasta is creamy and well coated. If you need to, you can add a splash of the retained cooking water to loosen things up.

Serve immediately with the grated Parmigiano.

MAKE-AHEAD PRIMAVERA RISOTTO

If you decide to make this dish ahead of time, it's best only to par-cook it (the rice should still be rather firm inside) and then spread it out on a baking sheet to stop cooking and cool. Finish the cooking process just before you serve.

1.3 litres/5½ cups vegetable stock

200 g/7 oz. mixed green vegetables (such as asparagus, green beans, broccoli and sugar snap peas) and mini carrots, cut into bitesize pieces

1 leek, thinly sliced

1 tablespoon olive oil

1 tablespoon butter

1 celery stalk, finely chopped

3 garlic cloves, crushed

350 g/1¾ cups arborio rice

100 ml/⅓ cup white wine

100 g/1½ cups grated Parmesan

3 sprigs of lemon thyme, leaves picked

a handful of parsley, roughly chopped

a pinch of chives, roughly chopped

a pinch of freshly grated nutmeg

a handful of fresh basil leaves

sea salt and freshly ground black pepper

SERVES 2

Place the stock and 250 ml/ 1 cup cold water in a large saucepan over a high heat. Cover and bring to the boil. Add the carrots and reduce the heat to medium. Simmer, covered, for 2 minutes. Add the mixed green vegetables. Simmer, covered, for 2 minutes or until just tender. Transfer the vegetables to a bowl with a slotted spoon. Cover to keep warm. Remove the stock from the heat and, if making in advance, set aside 100ml/⅓ cup (this will be used for reheating).

Add the leeks, oil and butter to a separate heavy-based pan and cook for 3 minutes, then add the celery and garlic and cook on a low heat for 5 minutes or until softened. Add the rice. Cook, stirring, for 1 minute. Add the wine. Simmer for 30 seconds. Add 100 ml/⅓ cup stock to the rice mixture. Cook, stirring, until the stock has been absorbed. Repeat with remaining stock, 100 ml/⅓ cup at a time, until all the liquid has been absorbed and the rice is tender.

If making the risotto in advance, remove the risotto from the stove and pour onto a baking sheet to stop the cooking and cool as quickly as possible. (The rice will taste a bit raw in the centre.) Refrigerate, uncovered until cold. The risotto can then be stored in a covered container for up to 2 days. Note: eliminate this stage if you don't want to make it in advance, and continue as below.

To reheat and finish cooking, return the risotto to the pan with the reserved 100ml/⅓ cup stock. Heat gently until the liquid has absorbed and the rice is tender. Add the vegetables, thyme, parsley, chives, a grating of nutmeg and 50g/¾ cup Parmesan to the pan. Stir. Remove from the heat. Stand, covered, for 2 minutes or until the vegetables are heated through and the cheese has melted. Season with salt and pepper. Stir in the basil and serve, topped with the remaining Parmesan.

PAD THAI

200 g/6½ oz. flat rice
noodles

4 tablespoons light
soy sauce

3 tablespoons coconut
palm sugar

1½ tablespoons
tamarind paste mixed
with 1½ tablespoons
water or
3 tablespoons freshly
squeezed lime juice

vegetable oil

100 g/3½ oz. pak choi/
bok choy, leaves
separated and sliced
lengthways

3 garlic cloves

100 g/1⅓ cups
beansprouts

1 fresh red chilli/chile,
deseeded,
½ chopped and
½ finely sliced

6 spring onions/
scallions, finely sliced

2 eggs, beaten

lime wedges, to serve

handful coriander/
cilantro leaves,
to serve

50 g/2 oz. cashews
or peanuts, roasted,
to serve

SERVES 2

On the surface, Pad Thai seems a relatively simple dish, in practice however, it is quite easy for it to turn into a congealed, under-seasoned, lump. The easiest way to avoid this is to keep a close eye on the noodles, separating them while cooking to avoid sticking together.

To make the sauce, place the soy sauce (or fish sauce if you're not vegetarian), coconut palm sugar and tamarind or lime juice in a small saucepan and place over a medium heat. Warm through until the sugar dissolves completely then remove from the heat.

Soak the noodles in hot water for about 5–7 minutes until tender, but not soft.

Put 2 tablespoons of vegetable oil in a large frying pan/skillet or wok over a high heat. Add in the pak choi/bok choy, garlic, beansprouts, the chopped chilli/chile and 4 of the spring onions/scallions. Stir-fry for about 1 minute until the garlic is aromatic, keeping an eye on it so it does not burn. Add

the noodles to the pan with 1 tablespoon of water, tossing them around and separating any noodles that are sticking together. Add in the sauce and cook, tossing occasionally, until the noodles have soaked up most of the liquid and are cooked through. Taste to make sure.

Push the noodles slightly over to the side to make way for the beaten egg. Scramble it in the pan and stir through the noodles. Taste, and if necessary, add more seasoning.

Plate up with the remaining spring onions/scallions, sliced chilli/chile, coriander/cilantro and cashew nuts sprinkled over the top. Serve immediately with the lime wedges on the side.

BUTTERNUT SQUASH & CAULIFLOWER LENTIL KORMA

This is a very cost-effective and colourful vegan tray bake, combining sweet but not too starchy butternut squash and cauliflower with lentils and spices. This is a mild vegan curry that will tempt reluctant vegans to enjoy a meat-free Monday.

2 red onions, cut into quarters

400 g/14 oz. butternut squash, peeled, deseeded and cut into 1-cm/½-in. cubes

½ cauliflower, cut into florets

2 teaspoons olive oil

60 g/¼ cup korma curry paste

200 ml/generous ¾ cup coconut milk

1 x 400-g/14-oz. can green lentils, drained and rinsed

1 lemon, cut into quarters, to serve

1 tablespoon freshly chopped coriander/cilantro, to serve

SERVES 2

Preheat the oven to 200°C (400°F) Gas 6.

Put the onions, butternut squash and cauliflower in a baking pan with sides and drizzle over the olive oil.

Bake in the preheated oven for 30–35 minutes until all the vegetables are soft and the cauliflower is also brown and crispy at the edges.

Meanwhile, mix the curry paste and coconut milk together. Pour the mixture over the vegetables and stir in the lentils.

Bake for a further 10 minutes. Squeeze over the lemon quarters, sprinkle over the coriander/cilantro and serve.

Serve with rice.

LEMON & BUTTER BAKED SALMON

*'Spring' and 'simple' are the words
that come to mind with this meal.
It's all about simple flavours and even
simpler techniques, and it celebrates
the flavours of Spring.*

8 new potatoes, cut into 1-cm/½-in. pieces
1½ teaspoons olive oil
1 teaspoon sea salt
8 asparagus spears, trimmed
10 cherry tomatoes
6 mushrooms, chopped into quarters
2 salmon fillets
40 g/3 tablespoons butter
2 lemon slices
freshly ground black pepper

SERVES 2

Preheat the oven to 200°C (400°F) Gas 6.

Lay the potatoes on a baking pan. Drizzle
over the olive oil and sprinkle over ½ teaspoon
of the salt. Bake in the preheated oven for
10 minutes.

Add the asparagus, tomatoes and mushrooms
to the sheet pan and stir. Bake for a further
10 minutes.

Add the salmon fillets with a large knob of
butter and a slice of lemon on top of each,
and sprinkle over the remaining salt and
some black pepper.

Bake for a further 10–12 minutes until the
salmon is just cooked. Serve.

BALSAMIC TEMPEH & CRISPY CAULIFLOWER

*What a treat tempeh is! A naturally-
fermented food which means it is more
nutritious and easier to digest than
modified and processed soy-based foods.
This balsamic tempeh is rich in flavour.*

2 tablespoons balsamic glaze
¼ teaspoon garlic salt
1 teaspoon maple syrup
2 tablespoons olive oil
1 x 200-g/7-oz. pack tempeh
½ cauliflower, cut into florets
½ teaspoon sea salt

SERVES 2

Preheat the oven to 190°C (375°F) Gas 5.

In a bowl, mix together the balsamic glaze,
garlic salt, maple syrup and 1 tablespoon
of the olive oil.

Wash the tempeh and pat it dry. Cut it into
16 squares or triangles.

Place the tempeh into the marinade and
turn to coat.

Put the cauliflower florets on a sheet pan with
sides, sprinkle over the remaining 1 tablespoon
olive oil and the salt. Make a space in the
middle of the cauliflower for the tempeh. Tip
the tempeh and marinade into the sheet pan.

Roast in the preheated oven for 30–35
minutes until the cauliflower is crispy at the
edges and the marinade mostly absorbed.
Serve immediately.

POKÉ BOWLS

Originating in Hawai'i here sea fish is at its best, the poké bowl is made with yellowtail or 'ahi tuna and is served as an appetizer. Now that the poké bowl has travelled outside of the islands, it has taken on a new life. It is popping up with an assortment of vegetables, noodles, pickles, tofu, and all things healthy and fresh. If you are not crazy about raw fish, then grill it for a couple of minutes on each side.

450 g/1 lb. very fresh sushi-grade ahi tuna
vegetable oil, if you wish to grill the fish
2 tablespoons toasted sesame oil
2 tablespoons tamari or soy sauce
zest and freshly squeezed juice of 1 lime, plus extra wedges for serving
1 tablespoon mirin
1 jalapeño, finely diced
1 tablespoon finely chopped pickled ginger
sea salt and freshly ground black pepper

500 g/2 cups cooked sushi rice or white rice
6 spring onions/ scallions, finely sliced
6 radishes, finely sliced
1 avocado, peeled, pitted, and sliced into wedges
1 Persian cucumber, finely sliced
sesame seeds, for sprinkling
Nori Komi Furikake (Asian seaweed mix)

SERVES 2

Rinse the tuna under cold running water and pat dry with paper towels. Cut the tuna into 2.5-cm/1-inch chunks and place in a bowl. (If you prefer the tuna lightly cooked, grill it for just a few minutes on each side until slightly charred but still pink in the middle, and then cut into chunks.)

In another bowl whisk together the sesame oil, tamari, lime zest and juice, mirin, jalapeño and ginger. Season to taste, pour over the tuna, and toss to combine.

Divide the rice between two serving bowls and top with the tuna, spring onions/ scallions, radishes, avocado and cucumber. Drizzle with some of the dressing and sprinkle with sesame seeds and Nori Komi Furikake.

Serve with lime wedges to squeeze.

LEMON CAPER MAHI MAHI

Mahi mahi (also known by its Spanish name, dorado) is probably the second most popular fish in Hawai'i, after 'ahi. Mahi mahi is firm and meaty, like a white version of tuna, and is similar in texture to swordfish. his is a deliciously satisfying dish guaranteed to please your tastebuds!

2 mahi mahi fillets
   (swordfish or
   sea bass work
   nicely too)
60 g/½ cup plain/
   all-purpose flour
3 tablespoons olive oil
45 g/3 tablespoons
   butter
4 tablespoons freshly
   squeezed
   lemon juice
2 tablespoons capers,
   drained
2 tablespoons chopped
   garlic
lemon slices and radish
   cress, to garnish
   (optional)
Hawaiian sea salt
freshly ground black
   pepper

SERVES 2

Cut the fish fillets into portions, approx. 5 x 7.5 cm/2 x 3 inches in size. Tip the flour onto a plate and evenly coat the fish on all sides.

Heat the oil in a frying pan/skillet over a medium heat. Add the butter and melt down until it starts to foam. Add the fish and sauté for approx. 5 minutes on each side or until lightly browned and golden.

Transfer the cooked fish to a plate lined with paper towels to absorb any excess oil. Leave any remaining butter/oil in the pan. Season the fish with salt and pepper and keep warm.

Combine the lemon juice, capers and garlic in a small bowl. Pour the mixture into the frying pan/skillet with the leftover butter/oil. Gently simmer over a low heat until the garlic is cooked through.

Serve the fish immediately on a bed of rice or salad and top with the lemon caper sauce. Garnish with lemon slices and radish cress, if you like.

Tip This sauce also works well with chicken or prawns/shrimp, served on a base of pasta, such as linguine.

DUCK IN ORANGE GLAZE ON A BED OF LEEKS & MUSHROOMS

This dish is a modern take on the heavy and sugary duck a l'orange of the 1980s. The duck combines with melt-in-the-mouth leeks and mushrooms. A fine dish!

freshly squeezed juice
    of ½ orange
3 heaped tablespoons
    St. Dalfour Thick Cut
    Orange Spread/bitter
    Seville orange
    marmalade
1 teaspoon red wine
    vinegar
2 boneless duck
    breasts, each about
    170 g/6 oz., skin on
2 large leeks, cut in half
    lengthways and into
    1-cm/½-in. slices
200 g/7 oz. chestnut
    mushrooms, halved
sea salt and freshly
    ground black pepper

SERVES 2

Preheat the oven to 190°C (375°F) Gas 5.

In a small bowl, mix together the orange juice, orange spread and vinegar, plus some salt and pepper, to create a glaze.

Lay the duck breasts skin-side up in a baking pan and spread the glaze over the top. Leave to marinate whilst you prepare your vegetables.

Put the vegetables in the baking pan alongside the duck and give the vegetables a good stir. Season with salt and pepper.

Bake in the preheated oven for 30 minutes, but baste the duck breasts once and stir the vegetables well to make sure they are cooking evenly. Serve.

SPANISH RED PEPPER & CHICKEN BAKE

This is a dish that tastes of Spanish holidays. It cooks whilst you plan your next summer vacation.

8–10 new potatoes, cut into quarters, lengthways
1 teaspoon olive oil
1 teaspoon sea salt
1 onion, finely chopped
1 garlic clove, finely chopped
1 red (bell) pepper, deseeded and very finely chopped
½ teaspoon marjoram or oregano
¾ teaspoon smoked paprika
1 x 400-g/14-oz. can chopped tomatoes
200 g/7 oz. mini chicken fillets
1 tablespoon freshly chopped oregano

SERVES 2

Preheat the oven to 200°C (400°F) Gas 6.

Put the potatoes on a small baking pan with sides, drizzle over the olive oil and sprinkle over ¼ teaspoon salt.

Bake in the preheated oven for 20 minutes. Make sure the potatoes are almost cooked. If not, give them a little longer.

Meanwhile, make the sauce. Combine the onion, garlic, red (bell) pepper, herbs, paprika, the remaining salt and tomatoes in a bowl. Add the chicken and the sauce to the potatoes, then cover with foil and cook in the oven for a further 20 minutes until the chicken is cooked. Sprinkle over the freshly chopped oregano, if desired, and serve.

MASALA LOBSTER

Need a recipe to impress? Well, here you have it. Because lobster is quite an expensive ingredient, this is a celebratory dish.

1 live lobster (or use a frozen lobster)

MARINADE
2 tablespoons vegetable oil
1 teaspoon Holy Trinity Paste (see below)
freshly squeezed juice of ½ lemon
1 tablespoon finely chopped coriander/cilantro
1 teaspoon salt
1 teaspoon ground turmeric
1 teaspoon ground cumin
1 teaspoon ground coriander
1 teaspoon dried chilli/hot red pepper flakes
freshly chopped coriander/cilantro, to serve
diced red onion, to serve
lemon wedges, to serve

HOLY TRINITY PASTE
200 g/7 oz. green chillies/chiles
200 g/7 oz. garlic cloves
200 g/7 oz. fresh root ginger
50 ml/3½ tablespoons vegetable oil
1 tablespoon salt

SERVES 2

To make the holy trinity paste blitz together the ingredients in a food processor. The paste will keep in the fridge for up to 2 weeks.

To prepare the lobster, the first thing to do is to cut the lobster in half directly through the middle. If the lobster is alive, you need to do this quickly and swiftly to inflict as little pain on the lobster as possible. The best way to do this is to use a very sharp knife and stab the lobster through the head. Lobsters naturally have a vertical line running from their head to tail, so use this as a guide and cut along this line. Remove the claws and legs from the lobster (if you are using frozen lobster, make sure it is fully thawed), hold the body tightly with one hand and pull the claws and legs away with your other hand. (The claws aren't required, but if you can, crack and peel away the shell to use just the meat.)

You should be left with two lobster pieces from the head to tail. Now you need to get rid of the gills (also known as 'dead man's fingers') and the stomach sac. The stomach sac and gills are both located directly behind the mouth. The gills look like cream-coloured, long, feathery growths, which aren't poisonous, but are very unpleasant to eat.

Mix all the marinade ingredients together in a bowl. Using a spoon, put as much or as little marinade as you would like onto the lobster halves. The marinade has a medium level of heat, so if you prefer it hotter, increase the amount of holy trinity paste. Once the lobster is marinated, place on a baking sheet, cover with clingfilm/plastic wrap and put in the refrigerator for a minimum of 2 hours and a maximum of 1 day.

Preheat the oven to 180°C (350°F) Gas 4.

Remove the clingfilm/plastic wrap and place the baking sheet in the preheated oven for 15–20 minutes. Check every 5 minutes to make sure that the lobster isn't becoming over-cooked.

Place the cooked lobster halves on a serving dish, sprinkle over the freshly chopped coriander/cilantro and serve with diced onion and lemon wedges.

APPETIZERS
& LIGHT BITES

SALT & PEPPER SQUID WITH LIME AIOLI

The good news is, you don't need a deep fryer to make salt and pepper squid at home. A frying pan/skillet or wok does the job. The bad news is these delicious crispy squid taste so good because they're cooked in lots of oil. But get the oil hot enough and these squid morsels will be surprisingly light and not at all greasy or heavy.

600 g/1¼ lbs. squid, cleaned
75 g/½ cup rice flour or cornflour/cornstarch
1 teaspoon Chinese five spice
1 teaspoon sea salt
1 teaspoon freshly ground white or black pepper
vegetable oil, for frying
1 long red chilli/chile, deseeded and thinly sliced
20 g/scant ½ cup coriander/cilantro
wedges of lime, to garnish

LIME AIOLI
2 egg yolks
1 garlic clove, crushed
2 teaspoons Dijon mustard
250 ml/1 cup olive oil
freshly squeezed juice and grated zest of 1 lime
sea salt and freshly ground black pepper, to season

SERVES 4–6

Begin by preparing the lime aioli. Place the egg yolks, garlic and mustard in a food processor and blitz to a paste. With the motor still running very slowly add the oil in a slow, steady drizzle until it forms a thick sauce. Stir in the lime juice, zest and 2 tablespoons of water. Season with salt and pepper to taste, then cover and set in the fridge until you are ready to serve.

To prepare the squid, cut down the 'seam' of the squid so it opens out flat. Pat dry with paper towels. Score the inside with a cross-hatch pattern then slice the squid lengthways into 2-cm/¾-inch strips.

Mix the rice flour, Chinese five spice, salt and pepper together in a shallow dish or plate. Toss the squid pieces in the seasoned flour to coat.

Pour enough vegetable oil into a frying pan/skillet or wok so that it has a depth of about 2½ cm/ 1 inch. Set over a high heat and bring to a smoking heat. Test whether it is hot enough to fry the squid by flicking some flour into the oil – it should sizzle vigorously.

Shake off any excess flour from the squid strips and fry in the hot oil in batches for 2–3 minutes, until lightly golden brown.

Remove the squid from the oil with a slotted spoon and drain on paper towels, while you cook the remaining strips in the same way. When all the squid is cooked, transfer to a large mixing bowl.

Add the sliced chilli/chile and chopped coriander/cilantro and toss the squid to coat.

Heap the squid onto a serving platter garnished with lime wedges and lime aioli on the side to dip into.

MUSHROOM-FILLED LETTUCE CUPS

Light and elegant, with pleasantly contrasting textures, these filled lettuce leaves make an appealing first course. Alternatively, serve them as a drinks party nibble. Fresh oyster or shiitake mushrooms would work well in this Chinese-inspired dish. Similarly, radicchio or chicory leaves, with their distinctive bitter note, could be used instead of lettuce.

1 tablespoon vegetable oil

1-cm/½-in. piece of root ginger, finely chopped

1 garlic clove, finely chopped

2 spring onions/ scallions, finely chopped, separated into white and green

300 g/10 oz. white/cup mushrooms, cut into 1-cm/½-in. dice

1 tablespoon rice wine or Amontillado sherry

2 teaspoons light soy sauce

1 tablespoon oyster sauce

8 even-sized Little Gem lettuce leaves

coriander/cilantro sprigs, to garnish

finely chopped red chilli/chile, to garnish

MAKES 8

Heat the oil in a wok or large frying pan/skillet. Add the ginger, garlic and white spring onion/scallion and stir-fry over a medium heat for 1 minute.

Add the diced mushrooms and stir-fry for 2 minutes. Add the rice wine or sherry and stir-fry for 1 minute, until cooked off. Add the soy sauce and oyster sauce. Stir-fry for 2 minutes. Toss through the green spring onion/scallion.

While the mushroom mixture is hot or at room temperature, spoon it into the lettuce leaves, filling each one with the mixture.

Garnish with coriander/cilantro leaves and finely chopped red chilli/chile and serve at once.

BROAD BEAN, RICOTTA & FETA CROSTINI

10 slices/strips pancetta
300 g/2¼ cups frozen petits pois
200 g/1¼ cups broad/fava beans
1 tablespoon olive oil
grated zest of ½ lemon
100 g/3½ oz. ricotta
10 freshly chopped mint leaves,
    plus 10 leaves, to garnish
salt and freshly ground black pepper
40 crostini (see below)
200 g/7 oz. feta, crumbled

FOR THE CROSTINI
2 part-baked baguettes, each sliced into
    30–35 slices about 5-mm/¼-in. thick
100 ml/scant ½ cup olive oil

MAKES 40

To prepare the crostini, heat a griddle pan on high and brush each side of the bread with olive oil. Cook the bread, in batches, for 1 minute on each side, until the bread is toasted and crisp. Place onto a wire rack to cool.

Preheat the oven to 180°C (350°F) Gas 4.

Cut each slice/strip of pancetta crossways into 4. Put the pancetta onto a baking sheet and bake in the preheated oven for 10 minutes, or until crisp. Set aside. Put the petits pois in a pan of boiling water for 1 minute and then plunge into cold water. Repeat with the beans and then squeeze them out of their skins. Put the petits pois and half of the beans into a food processor or blender. Blend together with the olive oil, lemon zest, ricotta, mint, salt and pepper. Spread a teaspoonful of the mix on top of each crostini, followed by a little feta, chopped mint, remaining beans and piece of pancetta. Serve.

MEDITERRANEAN VEGETABLE CROSTINI

4 tablespoons olive oil
1 red (bell) pepper
½ aubergine/eggplant, thinly sliced
1 courgette/zucchini, thinly sliced
¼ red onion, cut into wedges (optional)
1 x 125-g/4½-oz. mozzarella ball
40 crostini (see left)

FOR THE PESTO
50 g/generous ⅓ cup pine nuts
40 g/1½ oz. fresh basil leaves
1 garlic clove
60 g/1 cup freshly grated Parmesan
3 tablespoons olive oil
a squeeze of lemon juice
freshly ground black pepper

MAKES 40

Preheat the oven to 200°C (400°F) Gas 6.

To make the pesto, put the pine nuts in a dry frying pan/skillet and toast lightly over low-medium heat for a few minutes, shaking the pan regularly. Let cool, then put them in a food processor or blender with the rest of the pesto ingredients, and blitz until smooth.

Rub a little olive oil onto the red (bell) pepper and roast in the preheated oven until the skin blisters and turns black. Remove from oven, wrap in foil and, when cool enough, remove the skin. Slice into thin strips. Brush the aubergine/eggplant, courgette/zucchini and red onion (if using) with olive oil and chargrill/broil on high for 2–3 minutes on each side.

Divide the mozzarella ball into quarters. Then divide each quarter into 10 pieces. Spread half a teaspoonful of pesto onto each crostini, top with the mozzarella and vegetables and serve.

BEET & SALMON BLINIS

30 blinis
100 ml/scant ½ cup soured/sour cream
100 g/3½ oz. beetroot-/beet-cured smoked
    salmon, sliced into 30 pieces
freshly squeezed juice of 1 lemon
50 g/2 oz. lumpfish caviar

BLINIS (RECIPE MAKES APPROX. 80)
40 g/⅓ cup spelt
130 g/1 cup white strong/bread flour
1 tesaspoon salt
1 x 7-g/¼ oz. sachet easy-blend/rapid-rise
    dried yeast
150 ml/generous ½ cup soured/sour cream
175 ml/⅔ cup full-fat/whole milk
2 eggs, separated
30 g/2 tablespoons unsalted butter
a squeezy bottle

MAKES 30

To make the blinis, sift together the flours
and salt and sprinkle over the yeast. Warm the
soured/sour cream and the milk together in
a small pan until warm to touch then whisk in
the egg yolks. Pour the mixture over the flour
and yeast. Mix well, cover with a kitchen towel
and leave in a warm place. In a clean bowl,
whisk the egg whites until they form stiff peaks.
With a large spoon, gently fold them into the
batter. Spoon the batter into a squeezy bottle.

Heat a non-stick pan and, using a paper towel,
rub butter over the base. Squeeze 4-cm/1½-in.
blinis into the pan. They are ready when tiny
bubbles appear through the batter. Use a
palette knife to flip them over and cook briefly
on the other side. Cool on a wire rack. Top
each blini with ½ teaspoon of crème fraîche/
sour cream, a piece of salmon, a squeeze of
lemon and a little caviar. Serve.

QUAIL'S EGG, CRAYFISH & CAVIAR BLINIS

8 quail's eggs
30 blinis (see recipe on page 36)
100 ml/scant ½ cup crème fraîche/
    sour cream
60 g/2 oz. crayfish tails
50 g/1½ oz. salmon caviar
1 tablespoon freshly chopped/
    snipped chives, to garnish

MAKES 30

First, soft-boil the quail's eggs. Fill a small
saucepan two-thirds full with water and bring
it to the boil. Use a slotted spoon to lower the
eggs gently into the water. After 2 minutes,
remove and plunge the eggs straight into
a bowl of cold water.

Once cool, tap each egg on the counter and
gently roll to crack the shell. Carefully peel off
the shells and rinse each egg in cold water.

Slice each egg into quarters, lengthways.

Top each blini with ½ teaspoon of crème
fraîche/sour cream, a crayfish tail and a
quail-egg quarter.

Carefully top with a little salmon caviar and
sprinkle on some chives.

CRAB, CHILLI & LIME FILO TARTLETS

3 sheets of filo/phyllo pastry (135 g/4¾ oz.)
100 g/1 stick minus 1 tablespoon unsalted
    butter, melted

CRAB FILLING
400 g/1¾ cups fresh, cooked white crabmeat
5 spring onions/scallions
10 g/½ cup fresh coriander/cilantro
2 red chillies/chiles, deseeded 4 tablespoons
    mayonnaise
freshly squeezed juice of 2 limes
Tabasco sauce, to season (optional)
12-hole muffin pan, buttered

MAKES 40

Preheat the oven to 180°C (350°F) Gas 4.

Stack the filo/phyllo sheets in a pile and use
a sharp knife to cut them into 40 6-cm/2½-in.
squares, each of which will have 3 layers of
pastry. Keeping all other filo/phyllo squares
covered with clingfilm/plastic wrap to prevent
them drying out, take one set of three squares.
Lay one square onto a chopping board and
brush lightly with melted butter. Top with a
second square, offset to allow corners to
show. Brush lightly with melted butter and
repeat with the final square. Gently press
the layered pastry into the hole of the muffin
pan and repeat to fill the pan. Bake in the
preheated oven for 8–10 minutes, until golden
brown. Cool and store in an airtight container.

To make the filling, drain the crabmeat and
place in a bowl. Chop the spring onions/
scallions, coriander/cilantro and chillies/chiles
very finely. Mix with the mayonnaise and season
with lime juice, Tabasco, salt and white pepper.
Fill each tart with the crab filling and serve.

ASIAN SLAW & PRAWN TARTLETS

¼ red cabbage
¼ white cabbage
1 Gala apple, peeled
1 large carrot, peeled
1 spring onion/scallion
1 fresh red chilli/chile, deseeded
1 teaspoon salt
1 tablespoon sour cream or mayonnaise
17 cooked and shelled prawns/shrimp
34 filo/phyllo baskets (see above)

FOR THE DRESSING
2 limes
1 teaspoon caster/ granulated sugar
3 teaspoons fish sauce
2 teaspoons soy sauce

MAKES 34

Mix all of the ingredients for the dressing in
a bowl. Set aside.

Slice the red cabbage very finely and place
in a bowl. Shred the white cabbage, apple,
carrot, spring onion/scallion and chilli/chile
in the same way and place in a separate bowl.

Season both bowls with ½ teaspoon salt and
mix well. Add half the dressing to one bowl
and the other half to the second bowl, let sit
for at least 10 minutes but no longer than
30 minutes.

Drain the vegetables and mix together just
before serving so that the red cabbage doesn't
turn everything pink. Add the sour cream.

Spoon a little slaw into each filo/phyllo basket
and top with half prawn/shrimp. You can
pinch the ends of the prawns/shrimp together
to add height.

CRAB CAKES WITH SAFFRON MAYONNAISE

These crab cakes are ideal as an appetizer, or you could make a platter of them with bowls of the mayonnaise to dip into. The saffron gives them an earthy and moorish flavour, which is lovely paired with the tangy lemon.

300 g/10 oz., white
  crab meat
2 spring onions/
  scallions, finely
  chopped
small handful of fresh
  flat-leaf parsley,
  finely chopped
1 fresh red chilli/chile,
  deseeded and finely
  chopped
zest of 1 unwaxed
  lemon and 1–2
  teaspoons freshly
  squeezed juice
100 g/1⅓ cups fresh
  white breadcrumbs,
  can be from spelt
  bread or gluten-free
  bread
200 g/¾ cup
  mayonnaise
sea salt and freshly
  ground black pepper
1 teaspoon saffron
  fronds/threads
1 egg, beaten
sunflower oil, for frying
handful of rocket/
  arugula leaves
extra virgin olive oil

MAKES 12

Squeeze any excess liquid out of the crab meat and add to a bowl together with the spring onions/scallions, most of the parsley, chilli/chile, lemon zest, lemon juice, 50 g/⅔ cup of the breadcrumbs and 5 tablespoons of the mayonnaise. Season with sea salt and black pepper and mix everything together until well combined. Divide the mixture into 12 equal portions and form into slightly flattened balls. Refrigerate for 30 minutes.

Meanwhile, make the saffron mayonnaise. Place the saffron fronds/threads in a bowl and cover with 1 teaspoon of hot water. Give it a stir and leave to infuse for at least 5 minutes. Add to the remaining mayonnaise and stir to combine.

Dip the chilled crab cakes in the beaten egg and then roll in the remaining breadcrumbs until evenly covered. Set aside.

Pour 2.5 cm/1 inch of sunflower oil into a medium frying pan/skillet. Place over a medium heat until a piece of bread dropped into the oil browns in about 40 seconds. Carefully place the crab cakes in the oil and fry for 3 minutes on each side until crisp and golden. Remove with a slotted spoon and drain on paper towels.

Plate up the crab cakes with the rocket/arugula leaves twisted in and around them and the saffron mayonnaise on top. Drizzle over some extra virgin olive oil and scatter over the remaining chopped parsley. Serve immediately with lemon wedges on the side, if desired.

MUSHROOM PAKORAS

There is always something irresistible about deep-fried food! These Indian-inspired pakoras – made from nutty-tasting chickpea/gram flour and flavoured with fragrant spices – are a wonderful snack, ideal for a drinks party or as the first course of an Indian meal. Serve with a herbed yogurt dipping sauce or simply with lemon wedges.

115g/¾ cup chickpea/
   gram flour
1 teaspoon ground
   cumin
1 teaspoon cumin
   seeds
½ teaspoon ground
   turmeric
½ teaspoon salt
½ teaspoon baking
   powder
½ onion, chopped
200 g/6½ oz.
   mushrooms, chopped
2–3 sprigs fresh
   coriander/cilantro,
   chopped
vegetable oil, for
   deep-frying
lemon wedges, to serve

YOGURT DIP
4 tablespoons chopped
   fresh coriander/
   cilantro or mint
   leaves
200 ml/1 scant cup
   natural yogurt

MAKES APPROX. 12–14

First, make the yogurt dip. Stir the chopped coriander/cilantro or mint into the yogurt and set aside.

Place the chickpea/gram flour, cumin powder and seeds, turmeric, salt and baking powder in a mixing bowl.

Whisk in 120 ml/½ cup water to form a thick, smooth batter. Fold in the mushrooms and coriander/cilantro.

Heat the oil in a wok or large pan until very hot. Cook the pakoras in batches, dropping in a tablespoon of the mixture for each pakora. Fry for approx. 3–5 minutes, until golden brown, turning over each pakora as it fries to ensure even browning. Remove the fried pakoras with a slotted spoon and drain on paper towels.

Serve at once with the yogurt dip or lemon wedges for squeezing.

SHIITAKE POTSTICKER DUMPLINGS

60 g/2 oz. dried shiitake
  mushrooms
2 spring onions/
  scallions, finely
  chopped
1 garlic clove, finely
  chopped
2.5-cm/1-in. piece
  of root ginger,
  finely chopped
1 tablespoon rice wine
  or Amontillado sherry
1 teaspoon soy sauce
1 teaspoon sesame oil
salt
a pinch of sugar
22 potsticker/gyoza
  wrappers
2 tablespoons
  vegetable oil,
  for frying

DIPPING SAUCE
3 tablespoons light
  soy sauce
3 tablespoons Chinese
  rice vinegar
1 thin slice of root
  ginger, finely
  chopped
½ teaspoon chopped
  red chilli/chile or
  Aleppo chilli/hot
  pepper flakes

MAKES 22
DUMPLINGS

Dumplings are always popular and these are no exception! Dried shiitake mushrooms have a wonderful depth of flavour and here they are combined with spring onion/scallion, garlic and root ginger to make a truly tasty filling. Serve these as the first course of a Chinese meal or as a party nibble with drinks.

Place the dried shiitake mushrooms in a bowl and cover with freshly boiled water. Set aside to soak for 30 minutes, weighing down the mushrooms in the bowl if necessary to make sure they soften. Drain the mushrooms. Trim off and discard the tough stems.

Place the shiitake, half the chopped spring onion/scallion, garlic and ginger in a pan. Cover with water and add the rice wine. Bring to the boil. Partly cover and simmer for 45 minutes. Drain and cool.

Place the shiitake mushrooms in a food processor and pulse until finely chopped. Mix the minced shiitake with remaining spring onion/scallion, soy sauce, sesame oil, salt and sugar.

To make each dumpling, place a heaped teaspoon of the shiitake mixture in the centre of a wrapper. Brush the edges with a little water, fold over the filling and tightly press together to seal well. Repeat the process until all the wrappers are filled.

To cook the potstickers, heat 1 tablespoon oil in a large, lidded heavy-based frying pan/skillet. Add a layer of the dumplings, flat side-down. Fry for 2–3 minutes. Sprinkle over 75 ml/⅓ cup cold water, taking care as it will splutter. Cover the pan and cook for 10 minutes over a low-medium heat. Set aside and keep warm.

Repeat the process with the remaining dumplings.

Mix together all the ingredients for the dipping sauce and serve alongside the dumplings.

ENTERTAINING

CAULIFLOWER & CHICKPEA TACOS

1 red onion, chopped
2 garlic cloves, chopped
1 teaspoon paprika
½ teaspoon ground cumin
½ teaspoon sea salt
½ teaspoon dried oregano
1 tablespoon olive oil
1 small cauliflower
1 carrot
250 g/1½ cups canned chickpeas, drained

AVOCADO SALSA
100 g/3½ oz. whole green tomatillos
1–2 fresh green chillies/chiles, stems removed
2 cloves of garlic, peeled
1 avocado
1 teaspoon freshly chopped coriander/cilantro
1 tablespoon finely chopped onion
a pinch of salt

SERVE WITH
50 g/½ cup finely chopped white onion
35 g/⅔ cup chopped coriander/cilantro
12–16 flour or corn tortillas, warmed
6 radishes, thinly sliced

SERVES 6

The combination of cauliflower and chickpeas makes a healthy taco. These are easy to make, full of protein, taste great and the presentation of them looks pretty special too!

Preheat the oven to 200°C (400°F) Gas 6.

To make the avocado salsa, remove the husks from the fresh tomatillos. Place the whole chillies/chiles, garlic and tomatillos on a baking sheet and roast in the preheated oven for 6–8 minutes until all are slightly charred on the outside. Cut the avocado in half and remove the stone. Using a spoon, scoop out the avocado flesh and put it in a blender. Add the roasted chillies/chiles, tomatillos and garlic, coriander/cilantro, onion and salt and blend for 2 minutes. Up to 60 ml/¼ cup water can be added if it seems too thick. Add more salt to taste if required.

Place the red onion and garlic in a medium bowl with the paprika, ground cumin, sea salt, oregano, oil and 2 tablespoons of water and mix well. Remove the leaves from the cauliflower and cut it into small florets.

Peel the carrot and remove the ends. Cut the carrot in half lengthwise, then cut each half in two again. Slice into pieces that resemble small cubes.

Put the chickpeas, cauliflower and carrot into the mixing bowl and stir the mixture to make sure the vegetables are covered with the seasoning.

Spread out the mixture on a greased baking sheet and roast in the preheated oven until the cauliflower is tender.

To serve, mix the chopped onion and coriander/cilantro together in a bowl. Place a generous spoonful of the cauliflower mixture on each warmed tortilla and serve with the onion-coriander/cilantro mix, the avocado salsa and sliced radishes.

CRISPY PORK BELLY BLUE CORN TACOS

These are the most delicious tacos imaginable – slivers of crispy grilled pork belly wrapped in a blue corn tortilla and topped with an array of veggies. Hit it with freshly squeezed lime and hot sauce and enjoy with a chilled beer. If you can't find blue corn tortillas, use corn or flour.

900 g/2 lb. pork belly, skin off
2 bay leaves
60 ml/¼ cup white wine
1 teaspoon sea salt
1 teaspoon black peppercorns
198-g/7-oz. can chipotle peppers in adobo sauce
12 blue corn tortillas or yellow corn
oil, for brushing the grate

TO SERVE
lime wedges, lettuce, tomatoes, radishes, onions, coriander/ cilantro, queso fresco and hot sauces

SERVES 6

Place the pork in a lidded pan and add the bay leaves, white wine, salt and peppercorns. Pour in enough cold water (about 2 litres/2 quarts) to cover the pork by 5 cm/2 inches. Cover and bring to the boil over a medium-high heat, then reduce the heat and let the pork simmer for 1½ hours.

Place the chipotle peppers along with the sauce in a bowl and mash with a fork. Set aside.

Remove the pork from the pan and place on a cutting board. Cover and let it rest and cool for 10 minutes.

Heat the barbecue/grill to medium-high. Brush the grate with oil.

Slice the pork 4 cm/1½ inches thick. Using a pastry brush, coat both sides of the pork slices with a little of the chipotle mix.

Place the pork on the barbecue/ grill and cook for 2 minutes. Using tongs, turn the slices over and cook for another 2–3 minutes until crispy and slightly charred. Remove and place on a large platter.

Place the tortillas on the barbecue/grill and cook for a minute on each side. Remove to a plate.

Prepare the lime wedges, toppings and hot sauces and have your guests build their own tacos.

'AHI KATSU

This version of 'ahi Katsu, a Hawaiian dish with Japanese roots, is slightly fancier than the original local favourite, with an added layer of nori seaweed to give that extra umami element, but the recipe can just as easily be made without the nori and with pork, chicken, squid or another fish (such as mahi mahi/dorado or even cod or halibut) instead.

900 g/2 lb. 'ahi or
  yellowfin tuna fillets
1 tablespoon salt
1 tablespoon freshly
  ground black pepper
130 g/1 cup plain/
  all-purpose flour
4 eggs
100 g/2 cups panko
  breadcrumbs
8 sheets of nori
  seaweed
vegetable oil, for frying

FOR THE SAUCE
100 ml/⅓ cup light
  shoyu sauce
2 tablespoons dry
  mustard, mixed with
  a little water to make
  a paste
225 g/1 cup
  mayonnaise

TO SERVE
steamed white rice
furikake seasoning

SERVES 12

Cut the fish into slices roughly 18 cm/7 inches long and 2.5 cm/1 inch thick.

You will need three wide, shallow bowls. In the first bowl, mix the salt, pepper and flour. Break the eggs into the second bowl and beat them with a fork. Put all the panko breadcrumbs into the third bowl.

Wrap each fillet of fish in a sheet of nori so the seaweed overlaps. Lightly wet the tip of your finger in water and run it along the edge of the nori to help it stick and stay wrapped around the 'ahi. Dip each fillet into the flour mixture, then in the egg wash and finally coat with the panko breadcrumbs.

Shallow-fry the breadcrumbed fillets in vegetable oil over a medium heat, for 2–3 minutes on each side, turning frequently until evenly browned and golden. Place on a plate covered in paper towels to drain away the excess oil, then slice.

For the sauce, mix together the shoyu, mustard paste and mayonnaise and serve as a side sauce along with steamed white rice and furikake seasoning.

GRAIN-FREE TOMATO 'SPAGHETTI' BAKE WITH ROQUEFORT

175 g/6 oz. courgetti
(courgette/zucchini
thinly sliced using
a spiralizer or
julienne peeler)
175 g/6 oz. butternut
squash 'spaghetti'
(prepared butternut
squash sliced using
a spiralizer or
julienne peeler)
1 teaspoon olive oil
1 teaspoon sea salt
2 UK large/US extra
large eggs
330 g/11½ oz. tomato
sauce (recipe below)
12 pitted black olives
75 g/2¾ oz. crumbled
Roquefort

FOR THE SAUCE
1 teaspoon olive oil
1 onion, chopped
1 courgette/zucchini,
chopped
¼ teaspoon garlic salt
½ teaspoon sea salt
1 tablespoon tomato
purée/paste
1 x 400-g/14-oz. can
chopped tomatoes
1 teaspoon dried
oregano

SERVES 4

Spiralized vegetables bake beautifully and quickly, and create a great lower-carb alternative to the classic pasta bake recipe.

First, to make the sauce, heat the olive oil in a medium-sized saucepan. Add the onion and cook for 5 minutes until it's beginning to become translucent. Add the courgette/zucchini and cook for a further 5 minutes.

Add the garlic salt, salt, tomato purée/paste, chopped tomatoes and oregano. Cook for 10 minutes.

Pour the sauce mixture into a food processor and process to the consistency of a thick tomato sauce. Transfer to a small saucepan and keep at a gentle simmer over a low heat until ready to use.

Preheat the oven to 200°C (400°F) Gas 6.

Put the courgetti and butternut squash 'spaghetti' in a sheet pan or baking dish with sides. Drizzle over the olive oil and sprinkle on the salt. Mix well. Bake in the preheated oven for 10 minutes.

Meanwhile, whisk the eggs in a large bowl and then add the hot pasta sauce and stir.

Remove the vegetable 'spaghetti' from the oven, then pour over the sauce mixture. Any remaining sauce can be kept in the fridge for up to 3 days. Add the olives and crumbled Roquefort before serving. Place the dish under a medium grill/broiler to melt the cheese, if desired, and serve.

MUSHROOM MAC 'N' CHEESE

Served warm from the oven, a hearty dish of macaroni cheese is a perennial favourite. Here, the rich cheese sauce is flavoured with bay and mustard, and combined with a tasty mixture of fried leek, mushrooms and ham. A crunchy topping gives the finishing touch.

200 g/2 cups macaroni
 or short penne pasta
40 g/3 tablespoons
 butter
1 bay leaf
40 g/5 tablespoons
 plain/all-purpose
 flour
600 ml/2½ cups
 full fat/whole milk
125 g/1¼ cups
 Cheddar cheese,
 grated
1 teaspoon wholegrain
 mustard
freshly grated nutmeg
1 tablespoon sunflower
 oil
1 leek, finely chopped
200 g/6½ oz. button
 mushrooms, halved
100 g/3½ oz. pulled/
 shredded or diced
 cooked ham
2 tablespoons grated
 Parmesan cheese
25 g/⅓ cup fresh
 breadcrumbs
1 tablespoon pine nuts
salt and freshly ground
 black pepper
a shallow baking dish

SERVES 4

Preheat the oven to 200°C (400°F) Gas 6.

Bring a large pan of salted water to the boil. Add the pasta and cook, following the package instructions, until slightly underdone; drain.

Melt the butter with the bay leaf in a heavy-based saucepan. Mix in the flour and cook briefly, stirring. Gradually stir in the milk, mixing well with each addition. Cook, stirring, over a medium heat until the mixture thickens. Stir in the Cheddar cheese until melted. Stir in the mustard and season with nutmeg, salt and black pepper. Turn off the heat and set aside until needed.

Heat the oil in a frying pan/skillet over a low heat. Add the leek and fry gently for 5 minutes until softened, without allowing it to brown. Add the mushrooms, increase the heat, and fry briefly, stirring, until the mushrooms are lightly browned. Season with salt and freshly ground pepper.

In a large bowl, mix together the cooked macaroni pasta, the mushroom mixture and the pulled/shredded ham. Mix in the cheese sauce. Tip into the shallow baking dish. Sprinkle with the Parmesan cheese, breadcrumbs and pine nuts. Bake in the preheated oven for 30 minutes until golden brown on top. Serve at once.

AUBERGINE LASAGNA

A great vegetarian take on a much-loved classic pasta dish, this combines the satisfying texture of aubergines/eggplant with a fresh tomato and creamy white sauce. This is delicious home-cooked food with an Italian touch.

1 kg/1¼ lbs. ripe
    tomatoes
5 tablespoons olive oil
1 onion, peeled and
    chopped
1 garlic clove, peeled
    and chopped
salt and freshly ground
    black pepper
a handful of fresh basil
    leaves
2 aubergines/eggplant,
    finely diced
25 g/2 tablespoons
    butter
25 g/3¼ tablespoons
    flour
300 ml/1¼ cups milk
freshly grated nutmeg
about 12 cooked
    lasagne sheets
25 g/⅓ cup freshly
    grated Parmesan
    cheese

SERVES 4

Begin by scalding and skinning the tomatoes. Roughly chop, reserving any juices, and set aside.

Heat 1 tablespoon of the oil in a large, heavy-bottomed frying pan/ skillet over a low heat. Fry the onion and garlic until softened. Add the chopped tomatoes with their juices. Season with salt and pepper.

Increase the heat, cover and bring the mixture to the boil. Uncover and cook for a further 5 minutes, stirring often, until reduced and thickened. Stir in the basil.

Heat 2 tablespoons of the oil in a separate large, heavy-bottomed frying pan/skillet set over a medium heat. Add half of the diced aubergine/eggplant and fry, stirring often, until softened and lightly browned, then set aside. Repeat the process with the remaining oil and aubergine/eggplant. Mix the fried aubergine/eggplant into the tomato sauce.

Preheat the oven to 200°C (400°F) Gas 6.

Make a white sauce by melting the butter in a heavy-bottomed saucepan or pot set over a low-medium heat. Stir in the flour and cook, stirring, for 1–2 minutes. Gradually pour in the milk, stirring continuously to combine. Bring the mixture to the boil and simmer until thickened. Season with salt, pepper and nutmeg.

Arrange a layer of lasagne sheets in the bottom of an ovenproof dish. Put an even layer of the aubergine/eggplant mixture over the top, then sprinkle over a little grated Parmesan cheese. Repeat the process, finishing with a layer of lasagne sheets. Spread the white sauce evenly over the top, then sprinkle over the remaining Parmesan.

Bake for 40–50 minutes in the preheated oven until golden-brown. Remove from the oven and serve at once.

VEGAN BAKED FAJITAS

Fajitas seem like the best party food to serve to a crowd. Making up your own fajita whilst sat around a table with your friends or family is such a sociable way to enjoy a meal.

2 medium sweet
   potatoes, peeled
   and chopped into
   1.5-cm/½-in. pieces
3 teaspoons olive oil
2 (bell) peppers, ideally
   different colours,
   deseeded and cut
   into 2-cm/¾-in.
   long slices
2 red onions, sliced
   into thin wedges
1 x 28-g/1-oz. packet
   of fajita seasoning
   mix (try to avoid
   those with sugar as
   the prime ingredient)
1 x 400-g/14-oz. can
   chickpeas, drained
   and rinsed

AVOCADO MAYONNAISE
3 ripe avocados, pitted/
   stoned and skin
   removed
1 tablespoon freshly
   squeezed lemon juice
1 tablespoon apple
   cider vinegar
2 tablespoons olive oil
sea salt and freshly
   ground black pepper

SERVES 4

Preheat the oven to 200°C (400°F) Gas 6.

Put the sweet potatoes on a large baking sheet with sides. Drizzle over ½ teaspoon of the olive oil. Bake in the preheated oven for 15 minutes.

Meanwhile, mix the (bell) peppers, onions, remaining 2½ teaspoons olive oil and the fajita seasoning together in a bowl.

Once the sweet potatoes have been baking for 15 minutes, add the (bell) pepper and onion mix to the sheet pan and stir.

Bake for another 15 minutes then add the chickpeas for the last minute and stir well.

Serve with avocado mayonnaise, coconut yogurt and either wraps or rice.

Avocado mayonnaise Put all the ingredients, except the olive oil, into a food processor and process to a paste. Add the olive oil and process again. Adjust the lemon juice, vinegar and salt and pepper to your preferred taste. Serve.

PANEER KADHAI

This recipe is a north Indian, Punjabi-style dish that is an absolute winner for vegetarians. Paneer is an Indian set cheese similar to cottage cheese in texture but also quite like halloumi in regards to its firmness.

4 tablespoons
   vegetable oil
500 g/1 lb. 2 oz.
   paneer, diced
1 teaspoon coriander
   seeds
1 teaspoon ginger
   paste
a 2.5-cm/1-in. squared
   piece of fresh root
   ginger, cut into
   julienne
1 large onion, cut
   into 8 wedges
2 teaspoons salt
½ teaspoon ground
   turmeric
2 large tomatoes, finely
   chopped (core and
   seeds removed)
2 teaspoons tomato
   purée/paste

1 whole red (bell)
   pepper, deseeded
   and cut into wedges
1 whole green (bell)
   pepper, deseeded
   and cut into wedges
1 teaspoon dried
   fenugreek leaves
2 tablespoons freshly
   chopped coriander/
   cilantro (leaves from
   a small bunch)
2–3 fresh green
   chillies/chiles, sliced

KADHAI SPICE
1 teaspoon whole
   coriander seeds
3 dried chillies/chiles

SERVES 5

For the kadhai spice, toast the coriander seeds and chillies/chiles in a pan over medium heat until the spices become fragrant and aromatic. Blitz the spices in a coffee or spice grinder to make the spice blend, or pound using a pestle and mortar. (You will need 2 teaspoons of the spice blend.)

In a large wok over medium heat, heat the vegetable oil and seal the paneer on all sides. Remove from the pan and drain on paper towels.

Keeping the oil in the pan, fry the coriander seeds until they begin to sizzle. Add the ginger paste and ginger julienne and stir-fry until they start to brown slightly. Add the onion wedges and salt and stir-fry until they are cooked through but not too soft. This is a stir-fry dish, so you want the vegetables to retain a little bite.

Add 2 teaspoons of the kadhai spice blend and the turmeric and mix well for 1 minute. Add the tomatoes and tomato purée/paste and cook through until the tomatoes have melted and softened.

Add the (bell) peppers and 200 ml/¾ cup of water, mix well and cook through over low heat with the lid on for 3–4 minutes. This sauce base is a 'coating sauce', so it shouldn't be too runny. Add the paneer and fenugreek leaves and mix well.

Garnish the kadhai with freshly chopped coriander/cilantro and green chillies/chiles and serve.

GOSHT ALOO SAAG MASALA

Now this is a dish that stands out from the crowd – it is finished off with a lovely, rich, fresh spinach purée, which complements the beautifully tender lamb meat.

1 kg/2¼ lbs. leg of lamb on the bone, portioned into pieces
rice or naan bread, to serve

MARINADE
5 tablespoons vegetable oil
2 teaspoons salt
2 teaspoons Holy Trinity Paste (page 56)
1 teaspoon ground turmeric
1 teaspoon ground cumin
1 teaspoon ground coriander
1 teaspoon red chilli/chili powder
1 teaspoon garam masala
2 tablespoons natural/plain yogurt
1 teaspoon gram/chickpea flour

CURRY SAUCE
6 tablespoons vegetable oil
a 1.5-cm/½-in. piece of cassia bark
2 star anise
6 cloves
6 cardamom pods
1 teaspoon cumin seeds
1 tablespoon fine julienne of fresh root ginger
3 garlic cloves, thinly sliced
2 large onions, finely chopped
1 teaspoon salt
3 tablespoons tomato purée/paste
1 large tomato, chopped (core and seeds removed)
5 potatoes (Maris Piper or Yukon Gold, about 430 g/15 oz. in total), peeled and quartered
1 teaspoon garam masala
1 tablespoon freshly chopped coriander/cilantro
1 tablespoon freshly chopped mint
freshly squeezed juice of ½ lemon

SPINACH PURÉE
400 g/14 oz. fresh baby spinach leaves
1 tablespoon ghee, melted

SERVES 6

Combine all of the ingredients for the marinade in a large mixing bowl, add the lamb and stir to coat. Set aside at room temperature for 30 minutes, then refrigerate for a minimum of 24 hours.

To make the curry sauce, heat the oil in a heavy-bottomed pan over medium heat, add the cassia bark, star anise, cloves and cardamom pods. Fry for 1 minute to release the natural oils, then add the cumin seeds and fry for a further 1 minute.

Add the ginger and garlic and fry until light-brown. Add the onions and salt and fry gently until completely softened and golden-brown. (This may take 25–30 minutes, but be patient and allow the onions to fry slowly.)

Add the marinated lamb, mix well and cook for 30 minutes, stirring occasionally, to seal the meat.

Add the tomato purée/paste, stir in and allow to simmer for 3 minutes. Add the tomato and cook for 15 minutes or until the tomato completely melts into the sauce. Once the sauce has become nice and rich, add 1 litre/quart of water and the potatoes. Cover with a lid, reduce the heat and simmer for 30 minutes until the potatoes are cooked.

To make the spinach purée, put the baby spinach into a food processor and pour in the melted ghee. Blitz the spinach and ghee together until the mixture forms a purée. Set aside.

Add the garam masala, fresh coriander/cilantro, mint, spinach purée and lemon juice to the sauce and mix well. Remove from the heat and serve with rice or naan bread.

GARLIC ROASTED CHICKEN WITH SHALLOTS & CARROTS

Soft and succulent roasted chicken and sweet roasted shallots and carrots is a winning combination for a celebration meal.

500 g/1 lb. 2 oz.
  carrots, sliced in half
400 g/14 oz. shallots,
  halved lengthways
1 large garlic bulb,
  sliced in half
  horizontally
1.5 kg/3¼ lb. whole
  chicken
70 g/5 tablespoons
  butter or ghee
  (at room temperature)
1½ tablespoons dry
  white wine
200 ml/generous ¾ cup
  fresh chicken stock
150 g/5½ oz. baby
  spinach
sea salt and freshly
  ground black pepper

SERVES 4–6

Preheat the oven to 200°C (400°F) Gas 6.

Put the carrots, shallots, garlic and chicken into a roasting pan. Smother the chicken with the butter or ghee and season well with salt and pepper.

Roast in the preheated oven for 45 minutes, basting twice.

Meanwhile, place the wine and stock in a large saucepan and stir. After 45 minutes, add the vegetables from the chicken pan to this pan and remove the garlic. Squeeze the soft garlic pulp out into the vegetable/stock mixture and discard the skin.

Cover the chicken with foil and roast for a further 30 minutes, basting once.

Heat the saucepan with the wine, stock and vegetables in and simmer gently for the remainder of the chicken roasting time. Add the spinach and stir until wilted. Remove from the heat.

Check that the chicken is cooked through, then leave it to rest. Carve and serve the chicken with some of the cooked veg and a little of the stock over the top.

Serving Suggestion Serve with perfect roasted potatoes (page 117).

LAMB & MUSHROOM TAGINE

1 tablespoon
    sunflower oil
1 tablespoon butter
1 large onion, finely
    chopped
½ cinnamon stick
1 teaspoon cumin
    seeds
½ teaspoon ground
    cinnamon
½ teaspoon ground
    ginger
500 g/1 lb. lamb neck
    fillet, cubed
2 tablespoons tomato
    purée/paste
2 turnips, diced
2 carrots, peeled and
    cut into chunks
250 g/8 oz. white/cup
    mushrooms, halved
salt and freshly ground
    black pepper
freshly chopped
    coriander/cilantro,
    to garnish

SERVES 4

This slow-cooked lamb and vegetable tagine is simple to make and very pleasant to eat. Flavoured with a base of fragrant spices, the mushrooms are added towards the end of the cooking time and simmered only briefly so as to retain their firm bite. You can serve this with buttered couscous, quinoa or basmati rice, offering harissa on the side for a touch of piquancy.

Heat the oil and butter in a casserole dish or Dutch oven over a medium heat. When the mixture begins to froth, add the onion, cinnamon stick, cumin seeds, ground cinnamon and ginger. Fry briefly, stirring, for 2 minutes until fragrant. Mix in the lamb, coating well in the spices.

Stir in 900 ml/3½ cups water, the tomato purée/paste, turnips and carrots. Season with salt and freshly ground black pepper.

Bring to the boil, then reduce the heat, cover and simmer for 1 hour until the lamb is tender.

Bring to the boil again, add the mushrooms and simmer for 5 minutes. Serve at once, garnished with the chopped coriander/cilantro.

CROWD-PLEASER MEATLOAF & GARLIC BROCCOLI

8 slices unsmoked
 back bacon
2 carrots, roughly
 chopped
2 celery stalks, roughly
 chopped
1 onion, roughly
 chopped
2 garlic cloves, peeled
3 tablespoons freshly
 chopped parsley
800 g/1¾ lb. minced/
 ground beef
2 eggs
40 g/⅓ cup ground
 flaxseeds/linseeds
65 ml/¼ cup milk
1½ tablespoons butter/
 ghee/coconut oil
2 teaspoons sea salt
½ teaspoon freshly
 ground black pepper
1 head of broccoli,
 cut into florets
2 medium courgettes/
 zucchini, cut into
 2-cm/¾-in. slices
1 teaspoon garlic salt
2 teaspoons olive oil
3 tablespoons BBQ
 Sauce (no added
 sugar), such as Dr
 Will's, or balsamic
 glaze
33 x 22 x 10-cm/
 13 x 8½ x 4-in.
 loaf pan

SERVES 4–6

*What's not to love about a meatloaf? This one can
certainly feed a crowd. It's packed full of hidden
vegetables too. That's a win win.*

Preheat the oven to 200°C
(400°F) Gas 6.

Lay four slices of the bacon
in the base of the loaf pan.

Put the carrots, celery, onion,
garlic and parsley in a food
processor and finely chop.
Remove from the food processor
and put in a bowl. Mix in the
minced/ground beef, eggs,
flaxseeds/linseeds, milk and
butter/ghee/coconut oil as
well as the seasoning until
thoroughly combined.

Push the meat mixture into the
loaf pan on top of the bacon
and top the mixture with the
remaining bacon slices, tucking
the ends down the sides of the
loaf pan.

Bake in the preheated oven
for 25 minutes.

Meanwhile, put the remaining
prepared vegetables onto a sheet
pan with high sides, sprinkle
over the garlic salt and drizzle
over the olive oil.

Once 25 minutes is up, coat the
top of the meatloaf with the BBQ
sauce or balsamic glaze.

At this stage, put the vegetables
into the oven and bake both the
meatloaf and the vegetables for
a further 25 minutes. Toss the
vegetables once during cooking.

Serve the meatloaf and the
baked vegetables together.

7-HOUR LAMB WITH ROASTED CARROTS & CELERIAC

This succulent lamb dish requires very little preparation, but it does take a while to cook. The wait, however, is truly worth it. The earthy sweetness of the slow roasted carrots and celeriac complement the lamb perfectly. If you're missing some greens, you could stir some spinach into the juices once reduced and allow it to wilt before serving.

1 tablespoon sea salt

1 whole leg of lamb (bone in), roughly 2 kg/4½ lb.

1 tablespoon olive oil

4 large carrots, sliced into 2–3-cm/¾– 1¼-in. thick rounds

1 celeriac, peeled and diced

300 ml/1¼ cups dry white wine

300 ml/1¼ cups stock (meat or vegetable)

SERVES 8

Preheat the oven to 120°C (250°F) Gas ½.

Sprinkle the salt evenly over the lamb. Place a baking pan with high sides on the hob and heat the olive oil. Add the lamb to the sheet pan and sear on all sides until it reaches a lovely brown colour all over. Pour off the excess fat. Add the vegetables to the baking pan, ensuring everything fits snugly.

Pour the wine and stock into the baking pan. Put the baking pan back on the hob and bring to the boil over a medium heat.

Using oven gloves, cover the baking pan tightly with foil, then place into the preheated oven for 7 hours until cooked, basting twice during the cooking time.

Remove the lamb and vegetables from the baking pan, place on a warmed plate and cover in foil. Heat the juices on the hob again to reduce.

Carve the lamb and serve with the cooked vegetables and a little of the reduced juices over the top.

SPICY ROAST BEEF WITH BUTTERNUT SQUASH & CABBAGE

A spicy marinade really brings pizazz to this roast beef. Ideally, this should be served on the rare side for optimal flavour and texture. The butternut squash and cabbage really soak up the flavours in this one too.

850-g/1 lb. 14 oz. beef roasting joint
300 g/10½ oz. butternut squash, peeled, deseeded and cut into 2-cm/¾-in. pieces
200 g/7 oz. pointed cabbage, sliced

FOR THE MARINADE
2 teaspoons sea salt
1 teaspoon coconut sugar
1 teaspoon smoked paprika
1 teaspoon garlic powder
1 teaspoon mustard powder
¼ teaspoon dried marjoram or oregano
¼ teaspoon freshly ground black pepper
2 tablespoons olive oil

SERVES 6

First combine the marinade ingredients in a small bowl or ramekin.

Place the beef on a baking pan with sides large enough to fit the beef and the vegetables in. Rub the marinade all over the beef then cover with foil and leave to marinate for 1 hour at room temperature.

Preheat the oven to 200°C (400°F) Gas 6.

When the hour is up, add the butternut squash to the pan and roast both the beef and the squash together in the preheated oven for 1 hour 10 minutes, still covered in the foil to start with.

Add the cabbage with 30 minutes cooking time left to go and remove the foil. Give everything a good stir at the same time.

When the cooking is done, turn the oven off and take the beef joint out of the oven, then leave it to rest covered in foil, whilst the vegetables rest in the residual heat of the oven.

Once the beef has rested for 10 minutes, slice it thinly and serve with the vegetables.

SALADS
& SIDES

QUINOA & RED RICE SALAD WITH CASHEW NUTS & CITRUS GINGER DRESSING

This salad is perfect for a light lunch. Toasting the quinoa before boiling it in water gives it a lovely nutty flavour and helps it retain its texture.

2 medium red onions, peeled and cut into wedges, root intact
3 tablespoons olive oil
1 teaspoon brown sugar
60 g/⅔ cup cashew nuts
200 g/1¼ cups quinoa
200 g/1 cup Camargue red rice
100 g/⅔ cup (dark) raisins
2 handfuls of rocket/arugula
4 spring onions/scallions, thinly sliced
sea salt and freshly ground black pepper

DRESSING
5 tablespoons olive oil
1 tablespoon sesame oil
freshly squeezed juice and grated zest of 1 orange
1 tablespoon rice wine vinegar
a 5-cm/2-in. piece of ginger, peeled and finely grated
1 long red chilli/chile, deseeded and finely diced
1 garlic clove, finely grated

SERVES 6

Preheat the oven to 170°C (325°F) Gas 3.

Put the onion wedges on a baking sheet and drizzle with the olive oil, sprinkle with brown sugar and season with salt and pepper. Roast in the preheated oven for 25 minutes, until meltingly soft. Remove from the oven and set aside to cool completely.

Meanwhile, scatter the cashew nuts on a separate baking sheet and toast in the preheated oven for 8 minutes. Remove from oven and set aside to cool.

Once you have roasted the cashew nuts, spread the quinoa evenly on another baking sheet and toast in the oven for 10 minutes.

Set 2 saucepans or pots filled with salted water over a medium heat and bring to the boil. Add the red rice to one pan and simmer for 20 minutes. Add the toasted quinoa to the other pan and simmer for 9 minutes. Once cooked, both should still have a little bite.

Drain off the water in both pans using a fine, mesh sieve/strainer. Transfer the quinoa and rice to a large mixing bowl and set aside to cool.

To make the dressing, mix all of the ingredients together in a small bowl, using a whisk to emulsify the oils with the orange juice and vinegar.

Pour the dressing into the bowl with the rice and quinoa. Add the roasted red onions, toasted cashew nuts, (dark) raisins, rocket/arugula, and spring onions/scallions. Season with salt and pepper and serve.

PANZANELLA

Panzanella is a classic, rustic Tuscan recipe. Traditionally, it was made frugally with stale bread, given new life by being mixed with fresh tomatoes and flavourful olive oil. For best results, choose the ripest tomatoes that you can find.

1 red onion, peeled and very finely sliced into rings

100 ml/6 tablespoons white wine vinegar

2 teaspoons sugar

½ teaspoon salt

1 large yellow or red (bell) pepper

200 g/6½ oz. day-old rustic bread

500 g/1 lb. ripe tomatoes, ideally in assorted colours and shapes

100 ml/6 tablespoons extra virgin olive oil

50 ml/3 tablespoons red wine vinegar

1 garlic clove, peeled and crushed (optional)

1 teaspoon capers, rinsed

salt and freshly ground black pepper, to taste

a generous handful of fresh basil leaves

SERVES 6-8

First, lightly pickle the onion rings. Place them in a colander and pour over freshly boiled water. Transfer the onion rings to a mixing bowl and add the vinegar, sugar and salt. Pour over 150 ml/⅔ cup of water and mix together. Set aside for 1 hour, drain and dry on paper towels.

Meanwhile, grill/broil the (bell) pepper under a medium heat until charred on all sides. Place in a plastic bag (as trapping the steam makes the pepper easier to peel) and set aside to cool. Peel using a sharp knife and cut into short, thick strips.

Trim and discard the crusts from the bread and slice into small cubes. Cut the tomatoes into chunks or in half if using small cherry tomatoes.

Make the dressing by mixing together the oil, red wine vinegar, garlic and capers. Season with salt and pepper, bearing in mind the saltiness of the capers.

Mix together the chopped tomatoes, bread and roasted pepper strips in a large serving bowl. Pour the dressing over the mixture and toss together, ensuring all the ingredients are well coated. Add the pickled onion rings, then the basil. Mix well and set aside for 15-20 minutes to allow the flavours to infuse before serving.

SHAVED FENNEL SALAD WITH WALNUTS, PARMESAN & POMEGRANATE

4 tablespoons olive oil,
plus extra to serve
3 tablespoons freshly
squeezed lemon juice
grated zest of 1 lemon
15 g/¼ cup chopped
chives
½ teaspoon sea salt
freshly ground black
pepper, to season
600 g/1¼ lbs. (about
2 medium) fennel
bulbs, trimmed and
finely sliced
1 pear, cored,
quartered and thinly
sliced
seeds of 1 pomegranate
60 g/⅔ cup walnuts,
toasted
60 g/1 cup Parmesan
shavings
70 g/1¼ cup rocket/
arugula

SERVES 6

Using a mandolin to slice vegetables will transform your salads – courgettes/zucchini, beetroot/beets, fennel and carrots are all delicious raw when thinly sliced and dressed simply with lemon juice and olive oil.

Begin by whisking the oil together with the lemon juice and zest in a large mixing bowl. Add the chopped chives, salt and pepper to taste.

Add the sliced fennel and pear, and gently toss in the dressing to prevent any discolouration.

Add the remaining ingredients, one at a time, and gently mix together.

Serve with an extra drizzle of olive oil.

JICAMA, APPLE & FENNEL SLAW

Jicama is a wonderful bulbous vegetable commonly found in Mexican cooking. It has a crisp texture, similar to an apple, and is eaten raw in fresh summer and winter slaws or as a crudité. Yuzu is a sour Japanese citrus fruit, which is a bit like a cross between an orange and lime. It can be a little hard to find fresh but you can source bottled yuzu on the internet or from Asian stores. It is a useful pantry staple, to be used in dressings, drizzled over ceviche, or splashed into a weekend cocktail. You can substitute it with grapefruit or lime juice.

1 small jicama
4 red beetroots/beets
4 golden beetroots/
  beets/
1 fennel bulb
1 Poblano chilli/chile
60 ml/¼ cup bottled
  yuzu juice
2 tablespoons ponzu
  sauce
3 tablespoons mirin
2 tablespoons maple
  syrup
zest and freshly
  squeezed
  juice of 1 lime
small bunch of
  marjoram

SERVES 6

Peel the jicama and beetroot/beets and set aside.

Using a mandolin, one by one shred the jicama, beetroot/beets, fennel, and poblano chilli/chile and place in a large bowl.

Whisk together the yuzu, ponzu, mirin, maple syrup, and lime zest and juice. Pour over the slaw and toss to combine. Cover and refrigerate for about 30 minutes, to allow the flavours to meld together.

Tip out onto a large platter, sprinkle with marjoram leaves and serve chilled.

NEW POTATOES WITH BACON & MUSTARD MAYO

1 kg/2¼ lbs. new potatoes
200 g/1½ cups streaky bacon
20 g/scant ½ cup chives, finely chopped
20 g/scant ½ cup
flat-leaf parsley, finely chopped

MUSTARD MAYO
1 egg
1 garlic clove, crushed
2 tablespoons white wine vinegar
½ teaspoon caster/granulated sugar
1 tablespoon grainy mustard
2 tablespoons hot English mustard
½ teaspoon sea salt
300 ml/1¼ cups olive or sunflower oil

SERVES 6-8

Preheat the oven to 180°C (350°F) Gas 4.

Place the potatoes in a large saucepan or pot of salted water and bring to the boil over a medium-high heat. Cook for 20–25 minutes, until the potatoes are tender. Drain and set aside to cool. When cool enough to handle, cut in half.

Lay the bacon on a baking sheet lined with parchment paper and cook in the preheated oven for 15–20 minutes, until crisp. Remove from the oven and drain on paper towels. Chop into pieces.

To make the mustard mayo, place all the ingredients except the oil in a food processor and blend. With the motor running, add the oil in a slow, steady drizzle until thick and pale in colour. Mix the mustard mayo with the potatoes in a serving dish. Add the chopped herbs and bacon, and gently stir to combine, and serve.

MUSHROOM, PEAS, & SPINACH WITH HERB PESTO

3 tablespoons olive oil
1 garlic clove, sliced
8 portobello or large flat mushrooms
350 g/3 cups frozen peas, defrosted
80 g/1½ cups baby spinach
3 tablespoons pine nuts/kernels, toasted

HERB PESTO
20 g/scant ¼ cup pine nuts/kernels
10 g/scant ¼ cup fresh basil
20 g/1 cup fresh mint
½ garlic clove, grated
1 tablespoon freshly squeezed lemon juice
½ teaspoon grated lemon zest
25 g/⅓ cup grated Parmesan
3 tablespoons olive oil
½ teaspoon sea salt
freshly ground black pepper

SERVES 4-6

Preheat the oven to 180°C (350°F) Gas 4.

Heat the oil in a small saucepan set over a medium heat. Add the garlic and cook gently for 2 minutes. Arrange the mushrooms, stalk-side up, on a baking sheet. Spoon the oil and cooked garlic over the mushrooms, cover with foil and cook in the preheated oven for 10 minutes. Remove the foil and cook for another 15–20 minutes, or until the mushrooms are tender. Remove from the oven and set aside!.

To make the herb pesto, place all of the ingredients in a food processor and blend.

Slice the baked mushrooms into 5-mm/¼-inch pieces and put in a large mixing bowl with the defrosted peas and herb pesto. Add the baby spinach and toss everything together. Sprinkle the toasted pine nuts/kernels on top and serve.

VIBRANT BOWL OF GREENS

To make life easy, use the same large pot to cook the vegetables for this side dish. By putting them in the pot at different stages, they will all be ready at the same time.

2 small Romanescos, halved, or 1 larger Romanesco cut into 4 pieces
100 g/3½ oz. Chantenay carrots
200 g/7 oz. sugar snap peas
200 g/7 oz. green beans
100 g/3½ oz. asparagus

BLACK GARLIC & SAFFRON BUTTER
100 g/1 stick minus 1 tablespoon unsalted butter
2–3 black garlic cloves (or use normal garlic), roughly chopped
a small pinch of saffron threads, in 1 teaspoon warm water
sea salt and freshly ground black pepper

SERVES 6 AS A SIDE

To make the black garlic and saffron butter, grind the butter with the garlic, salt and pepper and the saffron in the warm water in a pestle and mortar. Store in the fridge until ready to use.

Place the Romanesco in a large pot of salted boiling water and cook for 2 minutes. Add the carrots to the same pot and cook for another 2 minutes, add the sugar snaps and green beans and cook for 1 minute, then add the asparagus and cook for another minute. Drain and place onto a serving platter. Top with some black garlic & saffron butter.

ROASTED VEG WITH PESTO & LEAFY SALAD

Keeping a batch of cherry tomatoes in the fridge can be very useful. They can really make a meal, whether it's breakfast, lunch, dinner or snack. On toast they are great with avocado, feta and rocket/arugula. Here, they are roasted and added to a delicious salad.

270 g/1½ cups cherry tomatoes on the vine
200 g/1½ cups mixed yellow and red romano peppers, roughly chopped
2 tablespoons olive oil
1 teaspoon honey
a pinch of chilli/hot red pepper flakes
sea salt and freshly ground pepper
a handful of rocket/arugula
1 tablespoon pesto (see page 116)

SERVES 6 AS A SIDE

Preheat the oven to 180°C (350°F) Gas 4.

Place the tomatoes and peppers on a baking sheet lined with parchment paper. Drizzle with the olive oil, honey, chilli/hot red pepper flakes and salt and pepper. Bake in the preheated oven for 20 minutes until just cooked through, then allow to cool.

On a serving plate place the roasted vegetables and all their juices, top with the rocket/arugula and pesto.

TWICE-BAKED CHEESY POTATOES

These potatoes are almost a meal in themselves and are delicious alongside a crisp salad and fresh tomatoes. Alternatively, enjoy a half-filled potato as your carbohydrate portion in your main meal.

2 large baking potatoes
40 g/⅓ cup grated/shredded
   Cheddar cheese
60 g/¼ cup soured/sour cream
½ teaspoon sea salt

SERVES 4 AS A SIDE

Preheat the oven to 220°C (425°F) Gas 7.

Pierce the baking potatoes lightly with a fork. Put the potatoes on the middle shelf of the preheated oven and bake for 45 minutes until tender.

Remove the potatoes from the oven and carefully slice in half. Scoop out the insides of the potatoes using a blunt knife or spoon, being careful not to slit the skin.

Mash the potato flesh with the grated/shredded cheese until the cheese is all melted, then mash in the soured cream and salt.

Put the potato skins on a sheet pan and fill the skins with the cheesy mash.

Bake for a further 15 minutes. Serve immediately.

PERFECT ROAST POTATOES

Who doesn't love a perfectly roasted potato? This could well be the best method of producing perfectly roasted potatoes. Give them a try and see if you agree.

2.5 kg/5½ lb. potatoes, such as Maris
   Piper, peeled and quartered lengthways
5 tablespoons goose or duck fat
sea salt and freshly ground black pepper

SERVES 6 AS A SIDE

Preheat the oven to 200°C (400°F) Gas 6.

Put the potatoes in a large saucepan, cover with water and add a little salt. Bring to the boil, then simmer for 8 minutes. Drain really well, tossing in a colander so all surfaces of the potatoes dry.

On the hob, heat the goose or duck fat in a sheet pan with sides (not one with a non-stick coating). Toss the potatoes in the fat. Season well with salt and pepper.

Continue cooking on the hob and once all surfaces of the potatoes are starting to brown put the potatoes in the preheated oven and roast for 40 minutes or until crispy. Serve.

SOUTH INDIAN RICE

South Indian-style rice makes a great accompaniment to the curry dishes in this book. The seasoned oil creates a wonderful aromatic depth of flavour.

200 g/1 cup plus 2 tablespoons
   basmati rice (rinsed)
50 ml/3½ tablespoons coconut milk
4 tablespoons vegetable oil
1 teaspoon channa dhal
1 teaspoon urad dhal
1 teaspoon mustard seeds
6–8 cashew nuts
1 dried red chilli/chile
12 large fresh curry leaves

SERVES 5

Boil the rice in 600 ml/2½ cups of water until it is three-quarters cooked and the water has nearly all been absorbed. Add the coconut milk and stir in well. Cover the pan with a lid, remove from the heat and leave to stand. The rice will continue to cook in the steam in the pan.

Heat the oil in a small wok over a low-medium heat, add the channa dhal and urad dal and move them around in the pan until they become golden-brown.

Add the mustard seeds and allow them to crackle. Remove the pan from the heat when the seeds have popped.

Add the cashew nuts, chilli/chile and curry leaves to the hot seeded oil and mix well. Be careful when adding the curry leaves as they will splutter and the oil will be very hot.

Pour the seasoned oil over the rice and serve.

STIR-FRY BINDHI

This dish is stir-fried, which means the okra retains its natural flavour and texture whilst garlic and ginger are used to enhance the freshness of the dish.

500 g/1 lb. 2 oz. okra/ladies' fingers
4 tablespoons vegetable oil
1 teaspoon mustard seeds
1 teaspoon cumin seeds
1 teaspoon fine julienne of fresh root ginger
2 garlic cloves, thinly sliced
¼ teaspoon ajwain seeds
½ teaspoon salt
¼ teaspoon black salt
½ teaspoon mango powder (sometimes
   called 'amchoor powder')
¼ teaspoon dried chilli/hot red pepper flakes

SERVES 4

Rinse and dry the okra/ladies' fingers, then cut in half lengthways. Heat the vegetable oil in a large wok over medium heat. Add the mustard seeds and allow to sizzle, then add the cumin seeds and fry until they have popped.

Add the ginger and garlic and fry in the oil until they become slightly browned. Add the ajwain seeds and toss in the hot oil for 30 seconds. Add the okra/ladies' fingers, the two types of salt, the mango powder and dried chilli/hot red pepper flakes, and toss around to cover the okra/ladies' fingers in the seasoned oil and spices. Fry until softened and the sticky substance that is released from cutting the flesh disappears. Cover the pan with a lid to help soften the okra/ladies' fingers if necessary; it should take no longer than 15–20 minutes to cook. Serve as a side dish.

BAKING
& DESSERTS

NO-KNEAD EVERYDAY BREAD

Impress your family and friends with a loaf of homemade bread. No special skills are required to make this crisp-crusted loaf with a chewy inside. Just follow the recipe and you'll do just fine. They never need to know just how easy this recipe is.

330 g/2¾ cups unbleached plain/all-purpose flour

2 teaspoons baking powder

60 g/½ cup plain wholemeal/whole-wheat flour

50 g/½ cup fine rolled oats

12 g/1½ teaspoons salt

240 ml/1 cup plain soy yogurt (thinner kind, if available)

225 ml/1 cup sparkling mineral water

2 tablespoons olive oil

FOR THE SEED MIX

2 tablespoons rolled oats

½ teaspoon caraway seeds

2 tablespoons sesame or other seeds

500-g/1-lb. loaf pan

oven thermometer (optional)

MAKES ABOUT 8 SLICES

Preheat the oven to 220°C (425°F) Gas 7.

Sift together the unbleached flour and baking powder, then stir in the wholemeal/whole-wheat flour, oats and salt and mix well.

In a separate bowl, mix together the yogurt, water and oil. Pour into the dry ingredients, mixing vigorously with a wooden spoon until you get a sticky dough with no flour left on the bottom of the bowl. The dough should be easy to spoon. If it's very thick and sticky, add 1–2 more tablespoons sparkling mineral water.

In order to get a nicely shaped loaf, cut a sheet of parchment paper to fit inside the loaf pan without any creases. For the seed mix, combine the oats, caraway seeds and sesame seeds, then sprinkle half over the base of the loaf pan. Spoon the dough into the pan, spread level with a wet spatula and top with the remaining seed mix. Press it gently into the dough with the wet spatula.

Put the bread in the preheated oven, lower the temperature to 200°C (400°F) Gas 6 and bake for 1 hour. Use an oven thermometer if you're not sure about the exact temperature in the oven. If you notice that the top of the bread is browning after 40 minutes, cover with a piece of parchment paper and continue baking.

Remove from the oven, allow to cool in the pan for 10 minutes, then tip the bread out of the pan, peel off the paper and allow to cool completely on a wire rack. This will prevent the bread from absorbing moisture and will keep the crust crisp.

Store the bread wrapped in a kitchen towel in a cool, dry place for up to 5 days.

VEGAN SUMMER MUFFINS WITH RASPBERRIES & BLACKBERRIES

325 g/2½ cups unbleached plain/all-purpose flour

65 g/½ cup plain wholemeal/whole-wheat flour

1½ teaspoons bicarbonate of/baking soda

1 teaspoon baking powder

¼ teaspoon salt

65 g/1 cup finely ground hazelnuts

25 g/3 tablespoons toasted wheat germ (optional)

420 ml/1¾ cups plain soy milk

200 g/¾ cup brown rice syrup

150 g/¾ cup sunflower oil

freshly squeezed juice of ½ lemon

100 g/1 small apple, peeled, cored and chopped

24 raspberries

24 blackberries

12-hole muffin pan lined with paper cases

MAKES 12

This is a very simple recipe for muffins that are juicy, fruity and a little nutty too! Adding toasted wheat germ gives them a nice golden colour as well as providing a little extra taste, minerals, vitamins and fibre. Find it in your local healthfood store and use it not only in baking but also in cereals, salads and smoothies.

Preheat the oven to 180°C (350°F) Gas 4.

Sift together the flours, bicarbonate of/baking soda, baking powder and salt in a bowl and add the ground hazelnuts and wheat germ, if using. Mix well.

Put the milk, syrup, oil, lemon juice and apple in a food processor and blend until smooth.

Combine the dry and liquid ingredients, and mix gently with a silicone spatula. Do not overmix otherwise the muffins will be tough.

Divide the cake mixture between the muffin cases. Gently press 2 raspberries and 2 blackberries into each muffin so that they are half-dipped in the mixture.

Bake in the preheated oven for 25–30 minutes.

Allow to cool in the muffin pan for a few minutes, then transfer to a wire rack to cool completely.

Enjoy the muffins on the beach, by the pool, on a picnic in the shade or wherever you like to spend sunny summer days!

BANANA BREAD WITH RASPBERRY LABNE

Banana bread is absolutely delicious on its own or toasted with butter but if you want an indulgent treat, try it with this beautiful Raspberry Labne. Labne is a strained yogurt which has a consistency somewhere between cream cheese and yogurt.

125 g/1 stick unsalted butter, softened
250 g/1¼ cups caster/granulated sugar
2 large eggs, beaten
1 teaspoon pure vanilla extract
250g/2 cups plain/all-purpose flour
2 teaspoons baking powder
4 very ripe bananas, mashed

RASPBERRY LABNE
150 g/1 generous cup fresh or frozen raspberries
100 g/½ cup caster/granulated sugar
500 g/2 cups Greek yogurt
1 teaspoon pure vanilla extract
a 900-g/2-lb loaf pan, greased and lined with baking parchment
2 fine mesh sieves/strainers, 1 lined with several layers of muslin/cheesecloth

MAKES 8 SLICES
and serves 4

Preheat the oven to 180°C (350°F) Gas 4.

Beat the butter and sugar together in a large mixing bowl until light, fluffy and a pale cream colour. Gradually beat in the eggs, one at a time, before adding the vanilla.

In a separate bowl, sift together the flour and baking powder.

Gently fold the mashed bananas into the wet mixture a little at a time, alternating with the sifted flour mixture so that the mixture doesn't split.

Transfer the banana batter to the prepared loaf pan, then bake in the preheated oven for 20 minutes.

Reduce the oven temperature to 160°C (325°F) Gas 3 and cook for a further 40–45 minutes until golden brown, firm to the touch and a skewer inserted into the middle comes out clean.

Set aside to cool in the pan for 5 minutes then turn out onto a wire rack to cool completely.

To make the raspberry labne, put 50 g/½ cup of the raspberries in a small saucepan or pot with the sugar and 100 ml/scant ½ cup of water. Set over a gentle heat and simmer until it reduces by one-third.

Remove from the heat and strain through the unlined sieve/strainer set over a mixing bowl. Discard the raspberry pulp, cover the syrup and set aside to cool completely.

Add the yogurt, cooled raspberry syrup, vanilla and remaining raspberries, and mix together. Pour the mixture into the lined sieve/strainer set over a mixing bowl. Draw the cloth together, twist the gathered cloth to form a tight ball and tie the ends with kitchen string. Suspend the wrapped labne over the bowl and set in the fridge for 12–24 hours. Discard the drained water and transfer the labne to a bowl, ready to serve with slices of banana bread.

STICKY GINGER CAKE

This is a deliciously moist cake. The spicy ginger flavour evokes memories of childhood Christmasses for some.

8 ready-to-eat dried dates

20 ready-to-eat dried prunes

75 g/¼ cup molasses or black treacle

100 g/⅓ cup maple syrup

185 g/¾ cup natural yogurt or use coconut yogurt for a dairy-free version

250 ml/1 cup milk (use coconut milk for a dairy-free version)

3½ tablespoons olive oil, plus a little extra for greasing

2 eggs, beaten

350 g/2½ cups spelt flour (or for a gluten-free version use 170 g/1¼ cups buckwheat flour, 100 g/¾ cup brown rice flour, 50 g/⅓ cup tapioca starch, 40 g/ 1½ oz. ground flaxseeds/linseeds)

2½ teaspoons ground ginger

2 teaspoons ground cinnamon

1 teaspoon bicarbonate of soda/ baking soda*

1 teaspoon baking powder*

* use gluten-free versions if looking to make a gluten-free cake

27 x 20-cm/10¾ x 8-in. brownie pan, greased and lined with baking parchment

SERVES 15

Preheat the oven to 180°C (350°F) Gas 4.

Put the dates and prunes into a food processor and process to a paste.

Add the molasses or treacle, maple syrup, yogurt, milk, olive oil and eggs and process again.

In a separate bowl, combine all the dry ingredients.

Mix the dry ingredients in with the wet ingredients to combine.

Pour into the prepared brownie pan.

Bake in the preheated oven for 30 minutes or until a cocktail stick/toothpick inserted into the middle comes out clean.

Remove from the oven and leave to cool a little before slicing into 15 squares before serving. Any leftover portions can be stored in an airtight container for a couple of days in a cool dry place.

COCONUT PAVLOVA WITH CHOCOLATE SWIRL CREAM & CHERRIES

This cherry ripe-inspired pavlova, with the combination of cherries, chocolate and coconut, is always a crowd pleaser. It can be made in advance but always add the toppings just before you serve. It also works well with strawberries if cherries are not in season.

MERINGUE

4 egg whites

250 g/1¼ cups golden caster/superfine sugar

1 teaspoon lemon juice

1 teaspoon cornflour/ cornstarch

1 teaspoon vanilla paste

100 g/1⅓ cups desiccated/dried unsweetened shredded coconut

TOPPING

400 ml/1¾ cups double/heavy cream

½ teaspoon vanilla paste

2 tablespoons icing/ confectioner's sugar

100 g/3½ oz. dark/ bittersweet chocolate, melted

1 punnet cherries

1 tablespoon coconut chips (optional)

SERVES 8-10

Preheat the oven to 150°C (300°F) Gas 2.

Whisk the egg whites in a mixer until they form stiff peaks, then whisk in the sugar, 1 tablespoon at a time, until the meringue mixture looks glossy. Whisk in the lemon juice, cornflour/ cornstarch and vanilla paste. Using a spoon, fold in the coconut. Spread the meringue in the centre of a baking sheet lined with parchment paper into a circle approx. 23 cm/9 in. diameter, creating a crater in the middle. Bake in the preheated oven for 1 hour, then turn off the heat and let the pavlova cool completely inside the oven.

When the meringue is cool, whip the cream with the vanilla paste and icing/confectioner's sugar. Swirl in the melted chocolate but do not incorporate completely – 2–3 turns with the spoon is enough. Spread it over the meringue, drizzle over any remaining chocolate and top with cherries. Finish with the coconut chips, if using.

CHURROS

Perfect churros come with practice. The exterior should be crisp and the inside chewy but light with air pockets. If you do not have a thermometer, measure 200 ml/scant 1 cup boiling water with 60 ml/4 tablespoons cold water.

½ teaspoon salt
200 g/1⅔ cups strong white/bread flour
¼ teaspoon bicarbonate of soda/baking soda
260 ml/generous 1 cup water at around 70°C (160°F)
400 ml/1¾ cups sunflower/corn oil for frying

FOR THE
DIPPING SAUCE
100 g/3½ oz. dark/bittersweet (70%) chocolate, chopped
120 ml/½ cup double/heavy cream
a thermometer
a piping/pastry bag

MAKES 30

Whisk the salt, flour and bicarbonate of soda in a bowl. Add the water and whisk quite vigorously so that there are no lumps.

Leave to sit in the bowl for 5–10 minutes, or until cooled and thickened slightly, while you prepare the oil.

Heat the oil in a small saucepan and bring to 180°C (350°F).

Spoon the dough into a piping/pastry bag (use a star nozzle/tip if you want ridges). Twist the piping/pastry bag and hold with one hand. Gently squeeze out the dough to a 5-cm/2-in. piece and snip with scissors into the oil, frying in small batches.

Fry for a couple of minutes and then turn over with tongs and cook until golden brown. Drain on paper towels and keep the churros in a warm oven.

There is no strict shape for churros. Snipping them into the hot oil in lines is the easiest way to get started. Once you get the hang of it, you can try piping them into other shapes, such as the horseshoes shown.

For the dipping sauce, place the chopped chocolate in a heatproof bowl. Bring the double/heavy cream to a simmer in a saucepan, then pour over the chocolate. Let it sit for 1 minute, then stir to combine. Serve the churros immediately, accompanied by the dipping sauce.

APPLE & BLACKBERRY ALMOND CRUMBLE

Almonds in many forms make a fantastic, more easily digested alternative to grain-based flours for many. They also provide great flavour and texture to dishes such as this delightful crumble.

150 g/1 cup fresh
  blackberries
1 eating apple, cored,
  cut into wedges,
  then very thinly sliced
⅛ teaspoon stevia
  powder
¼ teaspoon ground
  cinnamon
65 g/½ cup ground
  almonds
35 g/½ cup flaked/
  slivered almonds
45 g/3 tablespoons
  ghee or coconut oil
450-g/1-lb. loaf pan or
  small baking dish

SERVES 2

Preheat the oven to 200°C (400°F) Gas 6.

Put the blackberries and apple slices in the base of the loaf pan.

In a medium bowl, mix together the stevia, cinnamon, ground and flaked almonds and ghee or coconut oil using a spoon or your fingertips.

Tip the crumble mixture over the fruit in an even layer.

Bake in the preheated oven for 25 minutes. Serve.

Serve with coconut cream or cream.

BASIL & LEMON ICE CREAM

Coconut milk forms the base of this surprisingly delicious dairy-free ice cream. The sweet perfume of the basil leaves perfectly match with the sharper citrus juice and zest of the lemon.

800 ml/3⅓ cups
  coconut milk
55 g/¼ cup xylitol
90 ml/⅓ cup pure
  maple syrup
50 large basil leaves,
  roughly torn, plus
  a few baby leaves
  to serve
2 unwaxed lemons, zest
  peeled off in strips
  and 2 tablespoons
  freshly squeezed
  juice
pinch of sea salt
3 tablespoons
  cornflour/cornstarch
*ice cream maker
  (optional)*

SERVES 6–8

Pour ½ the coconut milk into a heavy-based saucepan with the xylitol, maple syrup, basil leaves, lemon peel and salt and heat through to dissolve the sugar. Place the cornflour/cornstarch in a separate bowl and very slowly whisk in the remaining coconut milk, 1 tablespoon at a time, making sure there are no lumps. Stir this into the saucepan over a medium-high heat until the mixture begins to bubble gently. Cook like this for a few minutes stirring all the time until it becomes noticeably thicker. To test, coat the back of a wooden spoon and run your finger through it – if the line holds and does not drip, it is ready.

Turn off the heat and leave for 20 minutes stirring now and again, then strain through a sieve/strainer into a bowl, squeezing the basil and lemon peel to extract flavour. Add in the lemon juice and combine.

Place parchment paper directly onto the surface of the mixture to prevent a skin from forming and leave to cool, then refrigerate until completely chilled. Once chilled, freeze in an ice cream maker or if you don't have one, pour the mixture into a wide flat (preferably metal) tray and place in the freezer. After 40 minutes or so, remove and use a fork to mix and break down the ice crystals. Repeat this process twice more.

At the final stage, blitz in a food processor to make it really smooth. Then return to the tray and leave in the freezer to set fully. Remove 15 minutes before serving to soften. Serve with a few baby basil leaves scattered over.

COCONUT RICE PUDDING WITH BLUEBERRIES & MAPLE SYRUP

This luscious and thick pudding is made using coconut milk and cream, and rice milk. For the toppings, feel free to use whatever you like. This version uses blueberries and maple syrup but Medjool dates and nut butter swirled through the pudding also works well.

150 g/¾ cup risotto
   rice, carnaroli or
   arborio
400-ml/14-fl. oz. can
   coconut milk
600 ml/2½ cups rice
   or almond milk
1 teaspoon pure vanilla
   extract
½ teaspoon ground
   cinnamon
good pinch of grated
   nutmeg, about
   ¼ teaspoon
pinch of sea salt
3 tablespoons pure
   maple syrup, plus
   extra to drizzle over
handful of frozen
   blueberries

SERVES 4

Rinse the rice thoroughly under running water and add to a pot with the coconut milk and rice milk and bring to a boil. Reduce the heat to low and simmer gently for about 20–35 minutes, stirring regularly to ensure the rice does not stick to the bottom. By this stage the rice should be cooked through with a thick and creamy consistency. Stir in the vanilla extract, cinnamon, nutmeg, salt and maple syrup and taste, adding a little more of anything you particularly like.

When ready to serve, ladle the hot rice into bowls and add in a few frozen blueberries (or whatever topping you choose), straight from the freezer. Drizzle over a little maple syrup and serve immediately. The blueberries will thaw out in the hot pudding, leaving gorgeous inky pools of juice as you eat.

MANGO & MINT KULFI

Kulfi is the Indian equivalent of ice cream and is a very popular and traditional dessert choice. It is meant to be denser, heavier and creamier than ice cream, which is why condensed milk is used, as it adds a lovely, rich and thick mouthfeel.

3–4 saffron strands
500 ml/2 cups full-fat/
  whole milk
100 ml/⅓ cup
  condensed milk
50 g/¼ cup caster/
  granulated sugar
2 teaspoons cornflour/
  cornstarch, dissolved
  in a little warm water
100 ml/⅓ cup double/
  heavy cream
200 ml/¾ cup mango
  purée
15 large mint leaves,
  finely chopped, plus
  extra to serve

TO SERVE
chopped pistachio nuts
dried rose petals

SERVES 6

Soak the saffron strands in 2 tablespoons of the milk.

Meanwhile, pour the rest of the milk into a pan with the condensed milk and sugar, and gently bring to the boil. Simmer for 1 hour, stirring occasionally so that the mixture does not stick to the pan.

Once it has reduced by half, stir in the dissolved cornflour/cornstarch, ensuring that there are no lumps, and whisk into the hot kulfi mix. Simmer for 2 minutes, stirring occasionally and making sure that the mix does not stick to the pan. Add the double/heavy cream and saffron strands in milk. Mix in well.

Remove the pan from the heat and set aside to cool until the mix is no longer warm. Test with a clean finger.

Next, add the mango purée and the chopped mint and stir well to distribute the ingredients evenly. Transfer to a pouring jug/pitcher and pour into the desired serving dishes or moulds (I like to use traditional Indian clay pots to serve the kulfi in, but glass tumblers work well too). Freeze for 2–3 hours.

Serve straight from the freezer, sprinkled with extra mint, chopped pistachio nuts and dried rose petals for decoration.

DRINKS

BEST EVER BLOODY MARY

A Bloody Mary is the ultimate brunch drink, allowing you to ingest booze before midday with complete legitimacy and even a hint of old-fashioned sophistication.

500 ml/2 cups tomato juice
30 ml/2 tablespoons Worcestershire sauce
30 ml/2 tablespoons Sriracha sauce
a 3-cm/1¼-in. piece of horseradish,
    finely grated
sea salt and freshly ground black pepper
60 ml/¼ cup freshly squeezed lime juice
300 ml/1¼ cups vodka

TO GARNISH
celery stalks
chilli/chile flakes

SERVES 4

Pour the tomato juice into to a jug/pitcher and stir in the Worcestershire sauce, Sriracha chilli sauce and grated horseradish. Season with salt and pepper, cover with clingfilm/plastic wrap and chill in the fridge for 30 minutes.

When ready to serve, add the lime juice and vodka, and stir well. Place a celery stick in 4 high-ball glasses, fill each glass with ice and pour in the Bloody Mary mixture. Garnish each with a pinch of chilli/chile flakes and enjoy!

POMINI

The tartness of the grapefruit juice works well with the Champagne as a refreshing brunch cocktail, kickstarting your appetite.

300 ml/1¼ cups grapefruit juice
1 bottle Champagne (750 ml/3 cups)
1 small grapefruit, cut into 6 small slices

SERVES 6

Divide the grapefruit juice between six Champagne glasses and top with Champagne. Add a slice of grapefruit and serve.

APEROL SPRITZ

The Aperol Spritz has a season and that is summer. It is a fun drink that is not too powerful and very refreshing. You can dress it up by adding flowering herbs from the garden.

crushed ice
1 bottle of Prosecco
1 bottle of Aperol
club soda
1 tangerine, cut into quarters
flowering herbs, such as rosemary or basil, or flowers such as lavender, pansies or honeysuckle, to decorate

MAKES 4

Fill four wine glasses with crushed ice.

Pour the Prosecco nearly three-quarters of the way up the glass, then add the Aperol (the ratio is three parts Prosecco to two parts Aperol). Add just a splash of club soda.

Squeeze the tangerine quarters into the glasses and decorate with flowering herbs or flowers.

APRICOT & BASIL MIMOSAS

This is a wonderful weekend brunch drink – light and fizzy with a herbal aromatics from the basil. Make the apricot and basil purée ahead of time (store it in the fridge for up to 24 hours) and when guests arrive all you have to do is add the chilled Champagne.

120 ml/½ cup simple syrup (page 157)
4 basil leaves
8 very ripe apricots, pitted/stoned
1 bottle of chilled Champagne

SERVES 4

In a small saucepan bring the simple syrup and basil to the boil over a medium-high heat. Remove the pan from the heat and let the syrup cool, allowing the basil to infuse. When cold, remove the basil.

Place the apricots and cooled simple syrup in a blender and process until smooth.

To make the mimosas, pour the apricot purée a quarter of the way up a chilled Champagne flute. Top up with the chilled Champagne and serve.

WATERMELON MARGARITAS

Look out for the yellow watermelons with exotic names such as 'Moon and Stars' or 'Yellow Doll'. They look exactly the same as the pink-fleshed melons but are a little sweeter. They make the most gorgeous coloured margaritas, especially when rimmed with Chilerito Chamoy hot sauce and Tajín-spiced salt.

2 tablespoons Chilerito Chamoy hot sauce
¼ teaspoon Tajín seasoning
1 tablespoon coarse sea salt
120 ml/½ cup tequila blanco
300 g/2 cups yellow watermelon chunks
small bunch of mint
60 ml/¼ cup simple syrup (page 157)
450 g/2 cups crushed ice
zest and freshly squeezed juice of 1 lime

MAKES 2

Pour the hot sauce onto a small plate. On another small plate, mix together the Tajín and salt.

Dip the rims of the glasses first into the hot sauce, then into the salt mix and set aside.

Pour the tequila into a blender and add the watermelon, four sprigs of mint, simple syrup, ice, and lime zest and juice into a blender and process until smooth.

Pour into the salted glasses and garnish with a mint sprig.

MARGARITAS WITH JALAPEÑOS

This classic drink is definitely great for a crowd! Refreshing with a touch of heat from the addition of the jalapeño pepper.

300 ml/1¼ cups tequila
juice from 6 limes, plus 2 limes
   cut into wedges, to serve
3 tablespoons agave syrup
5 cups ice cubes
3 tablespoons fine sea salt
1 jalapeño, sliced

SERVES 6

Put the tequila, lime juice, agave syrup and ice in a blender and blend until smooth. Pour the salt onto a plate and moisten the rims of 6 glasses with a lime wedge. Dip the rim of each glass into the salt and pour in the margaritas. Serve with lime wedges and a slice of jalapeño in each glass.

PISCO SOURS

The Pisco Sour originates in Lima and it could be considered Peru's national drink. Pisco – a spirit distilled from grapes – has a bright, lively flavour with grape aromatics. Invest in a good Pisco as it makes all the difference. Mixed with lime, it makes a really nice cocktail to be sipped slowly as the sun goes down.

ice cubes
120 ml/½ cup Pisco
60 ml/¼ cup freshly squeezed lime juice
2 egg whites
3 tablespoons simple syrup (see below)
dash of angostura bitters
lime wheels, to garnish

SIMPLE SYRUP
200 g/1 cup white sugar

MAKES 2

To make the simple syrup, put the sugar and 250 ml/1 cup water in a saucepan and bring to the boil over a medium-high heat. Reduce the heat and simmer until the sugar has dissolved. Remove from the heat and cool. This makes approx. 250 ml/1 cup. Store in a jar with a lid in the fridge.

Fill a cocktail shaker with ice and pour in the Pisco, lime juice, egg whites and simple syrup. Shake vigorously and strain into two glasses.

Top with a dash of angostura bitters and garnish with lime wheels.

CUCUMBER MARTINI

This cocktail is so refreshing and is wonderful served up as a cooler on a warm summer's evening.

1 Persian cucumber, peeled and chopped
2 tablespoons simple syrup (see left)
6 mint leaves
1 tablespoon freshly squeezed lemon juice
ice cubes
60 ml/¼ cup vodka
fennel flowers, to decorate (optional)

SERVES 2

Place the cucumber, simple syrup, mint leaves and lemon juice in a blender and process until smooth.

Fill a cocktail shaker with ice and pour in the cucumber mix, along with the vodka. Shake vigorously and pour into chilled glasses, then decorate with fennel flowers, if using.

INDEX